Fo

Mom, Does God Know We're in Wyoming?

C. Ellen Watts

Ps. 139

Mom, Does God Know We're in Wyoming?

C. Ellen Watts

Pleasant Word
A Division of WINEPRESS PUBLISHING

Pleasant Word (a division of WinePress Publishing, PO Box 428, Enumclaw, WA 98022) functions only as book publisher. As such, the ultimate design, content, editorial accuracy, and views expressed or implied in this work are those of the author.

ISBN 1-4141-0524-X
Library of Congress Catalog Card Number: 2005907497

Dedication

For the five who call me Mom—
Anita, Jennifer, Kristin, Andrea, and Renee.

Love came to us in little girl packages.
Released from childhood's wrappings,
each daughter became a special friend.

Table of Contents

Preface

I knew the day I opened my Bible and found Psalms glued to Proverbs with sneezed droplets of Gerber's that babies and Bible study make a poor mix. With five clamoring daily for slices of my attention, prolific parenthood also meant that prayer too often happened only in emergencies or if I could keep my eyelids propped after all kid lids had fallen shut. God, I think, placed five in our quiver for two reasons: parents learn from their children and "women will be saved through childbearing" (1 Timothy 2:15, NIV)

My new life in Christ—a journey that began shortly before the birth of our first child—might have gone more smoothly had I realized a multi-task God understands more about motherhood than we who claim the distinction. Or that He would gladly have cheered me on had I embarked on my Christian walk with the confidence demonstrated at toddle time by our third-born. While the urge to make tracks with her own two feet began at a different age for each of our five daughters, the two closest in age staggered from floor mop to mobility stage in totally opposite ways.

Chafed by nickel-sized chicken pox beneath her diaper, the tall one made no attempt to walk at eleven months, as had our firstborn. At thirteen months, she lost her balance over the searing grate covering an old-fashioned floor furnace, burning twin red checkerboards onto the backs of her plump upper legs. From that blustery March night forward, to walk was out of the question.

Come summer, as I waddled into August to begin the final sweltering weeks of a third pregnancy, I wondered. Was obstetrical history to be forged by my giving birth with a wouldn't-be toddler astraddle one hip? Three weeks prior to due date, I issued an ultimatum. Either Miss Persistence could take herself off what remained of my lap and get on with the business of walking, or she could sit on her fears and whine until all her friends sailed off on graduation cruises. Four days later, as if a secret timer had gone off, she picked her paling pink checkerboards up off the floor and walked!

Having listened for months from the safer side of the womb, hearing me beg and bargain with her sister, the new babe met toddle time with serendipitous aplomb. She was but ten months old the night I lifted her from her bath in our old-fashioned kitchen sink, dried her and, with her daddy's help, coaxed her into taking a few steps between our outstretched hands. The evening being warm for June, we then turned her loose to "play in her skin" (our curly-haired one's term for running stark naked through the house while yelling at the top of her lungs).

As we watched, the short one took two steps and plopped forward. Landing hands first, she righted herself, teetered for a moment, and then toddled nonstop past the dining area table and on into the living room. Lifting dimpled hands, she smacked the front door, turned, and grinned back at us. Toddling back to the kitchen, spurred on by shouts from her sisters, she twice repeated the act. After the doting way of young parents, we clapped and laughed and encouraged her until I finally caught her and snuggled those newly animated legs into pink kitten pajamas.

For more busy years than I care to count, my walk with Christ paralleled that of the tall one's failure even to attempt a few steps. Frequent absence from the classroom of the One who sought daily to encourage me raised blisters in the form of troubles that might well have formed scars of indifference. God, however, quietly continued with his lesson plan, teaching me through circumstances and other people, and with audacious creativity, through my own children.

The following stories are reminiscent of that innovative classroom where, busy fixing dinner or not, I learned one step at a time to walk with Jesus. I pray that you will learn from them too.

—C. Ellen Watts

Acknowledgments

I am grateful to my daughters, Anita, Jennifer, Kristin, Andrea, and Renee for the fun and (sometimes) scary ways they once found to insure my spiritual growth, and for the lessons I am still learning from them. I thank each one for the many times they have graciously forgiven their imperfect mom and for all the years of waiting in silence for Mom to look up from the keyboard. All five have given me grandchildren and all have entrusted me with their reputations in the making of this book. What more could a mother ask?

My husband and best friend, Norm, has been my encourager. His loving support has helped to make this book possible. While the book is correct in picturing him as often out of town, he was never an absentee husband or father. I could not have molded and mentored out children without him.

To friendly editor, David Nadeau, project managers, Tammy Hopf and Tim Noreen, publicist, Lisa Rusicka, and all the other good folks at Pleasant Word—thanks for your hard work and for believing in this project.

Special thanks to Jill Nogales, Kathryn Johnson, Jan McNaught, J. Melton Thomas and the many, many others who have encouraged me along the way.

Chapter 1

Chute!

Jesus called the crowd to him and said, "Listen and understand. What goes into a man's mouth does not make him 'unclean,' but what comes out of his mouth, that is what makes him 'unclean.'"

—Matthew 15:10, NIV

It was one of those Saturdays. Chores ran rampant along with the kids. The man beside whom I had so willingly (albeit unsuspectingly) said "I do" had to work. When Ruthie walked in without knocking and invited Anita, our five-year-old, for a day of play that included lunch, I did a little soft shoe across a jelly-dappled floor and quickly dropped my mop. Giving my hair a pat, I escorted both inviter and invitee across the street and onto the veranda of the big yellow two-story before the folks closest to Ruthie could change either their address or their minds. Yes, the visit was OK with Ruthie's parents; it had been their idea in fact.

Concerning moms with large families: most days our love for kids is equal to and/or may even excel that of mothers of 1.6 (or however many children current statistics report per average household). Further, any space occupied by happy children is space coveted by other kids. Born through no fault of her own into a 1.0 child family, to Ruthie, our (at the time) 3.0 kid yard must have looked like a clone of Disneyland with no ticket required. An invitation for one of our brood to play at Ruthie's in return for Ruthie's daily breakfast-to-bedtime visits to our house and yard was highly irregular.

So, as it turned out, was Anita's day at Ruthie's.

With no one home to tattle on the two toddlers dumping sand in each other's hair, I whipped through chores in record time and was peeling potatoes for Saturday night's soup and Sunday's potato salad when Kris pressed her wee nose through a hole in the back screen door.

"Sissy's brack," she announced.

"Mm," I murmured. "You three have fun."

She disappeared behind the garage; then it hit me. In her typical toddler vocabulary, *R* nearly always replaced *L*.

Black?

Before I could program *black* into an English-Irish family, the one who had been with Ruthie all day skipped up the back steps and slammed into the house. Grabbing me around what I suppose still passed for a waist, she exclaimed, "Ruthie gots the neatest slide. You have to climb in a really skinny window—like this—Ruthie's taking a bath."

Chute!

Staring at the blackened face grinning up at me, I moaned. Hair that had been honey blonde and a once-pink T-shirt suggested a story I wasn't sure I wanted to hear. Touching a baby-soft cheek, I examined my fingertip.

"Ruthie's not s'posed to play in the coal chute," she said, at the same time telling on herself.

Let these two facts go on record: bar soap is to coal scum as water is to spilled oil along an Alaska coastline. Where coal dust is involved, shampoo cleanses hair, does little for scalp, and nothing at all for ears.

Hands gray with coal scum, I reached for the ringing telephone and listened to Ruthie's mother explain, "We were painting the kitchen. They were where we could hear them and they sounded so happy...Have you any idea what might take this stuff off?"

"No, dear. However, I have cleaned cream from beneath both stove and refrigerator—cream, along with splintered glass from a jar dropped by a two-year-old. I have rescued a dust-covered fantail fish from the bowels of a hot air register, witnessed said fantail's survival and..."

Mothers of 1.0 offspring probably had time to watch an only child more closely than did mothers of 3.0 children, I concluded as I waited through the brief silence that followed.

Struck suddenly by a terrific idea, I blurted, "The kids have this book about Grady the cow. She got stuck in a silo."

More silence.

"We've read the story a jillion times."

"Um."

"They smeared Grady with Crisco—you know—vegetable shortening. She popped right out. It's a true story. I think it happened in Iowa."

"I see."

She didn't, but I couldn't let that bother me. "We could use shortening—you know—like we use cold cream for removing makeup."

A half-can of Crisco and one giant roll of paper towels later, much of the coal grime had been transferred to the wastebasket. Lacing warm bath water with a liberal dose of dishwashing liquid, I proceeded to sponge off Crisco.

When soapsuds accidentally got in her mouth, the curly-haired one giggled. "Yuk. I'm glad I'm clean inside so I don't have to *drink* soap!"

She was in her pajamas, jabbing celery into a bowl of potato soup crammed with smashed saltines before she remembered to ask, "Are you mad at me, Mommy?"

The worst being history, I smiled. "No."

Rosier-than-usual chin in hand, her clean elbow propped against the table, she sighed, "It was so much fun."

How could I be mad at her? She had not disobeyed. Besides, as one commissioned to be salt and light to a world peppered with sin, I sometimes rub shoulders with folks for whom the Grady cow plan is never going to work. Might be that the coal chute story could become a springboard for sharing the good news of Jesus Christ and how willing He is to clean up a life and help set folks on the right path. Such retelling might even prevent a few from attempting to suds away sin by guzzling dish soap.

Lord, may the lessons that come so often to me through my children stick tighter than coal dust in a wee pink ear.

Chapter 2

Tiptoe Due to Tulips

The Lord said to Moses, "Say to the Israelites: 'When a man or woman wrongs another in any way and so is unfaithful to the Lord, that person is guilty and must confess the sin he has committed. He must make full restitution for his wrong.'"

—Numbers 5:6-7a, NIV

Possibly, my morning agenda was important. Could be yours truly was simply experiencing another of her dumb mom days. Either way, even the least skilled among mothers should have known that to send a two-year-old out to play with a three-year-old while the mother of said two-year-old is occupied with leading a serious Bible study was, still is, and forever will be a no-no. For sure, the toddler bearing my last name ought to have received more than a glance when she interrupted Paul's letter to the Colossians to show off the green lumps of wonder filling the bottom of her last summer's sand pail.

Instead, placing a finger on my notes, pointing with another to the door, I murmured, "Nice, honey. Now run back out and play with Tommy," and spoke blissfully on to the small group of ladies gracing our rental house living room.

Later, after both Tommy and the ladies had gone, I stepped out the back door to collect our toddler for lunch and a nap. The sand pail sat abandoned in the middle of a back step. Curious over the green that now reached nearly to its scratched orange rim, I crossed the patio, took one look and, for a moment, lost my grasp on all four gospels and most of the rest of the New Testament.

Recalling in the nick of time Paul's words concerning gentleness and patience, I said to the small one, "Andie, can you please show Mommy where you found these?"

While I considered the feasibility of simply disappearing beneath the roots of the giant oak tree growing between our house and the neighbor's, the owner of the bucket grabbed my hand with her busy little fingers and led me to where I already knew I did not want to go.

Through the bay window of the dining room in the house beyond our driveway, I could see the back of a stylish blue perm worn by one of three ladies who lunched each Tuesday with our widowed next-door neighbor, then stayed to play bridge. On the slope beneath the window, the bud-less stems of a thousand (more or less) would-have-been tulips offered evidence enough to warrant the blade of a guillotine designed specifically for impeachable mothers.

"Tommy hold 'e bucket, I pick 'e baws," jabbered the one whose left hand could not possibly have understood the crime committed by her right. In her present vocabulary, anything remotely resembling a sphere was a "ball."

Why, oh, why had I not paid attention to my offspring while a portion of the bottom of that rusty little pail still showed?

The bridge club lingered longer than usual, buying me a little bit of time. A sympathetic florist whipped out a fabulous basket of blooming tulips. Her empathy (she too had mothered a two-year-old) made it a tad easier to drag my dingy sneakers three car-lengths along our elm-shaded sidewalk and onto the neatly swept porch next door.

Had it been May, I might have dropped that $40 tulip arrangement, hollered "May basket!" through the keyhole, and run like crazy. But it was April. I rang the doorbell.

Eternity grew sideburns and a beard before my neighbor at last opened her door. Forever after I would remember thinking how an understanding God must surely have arranged for her attire. Instead of her usual tailored and somewhat formidable garb, she had thrust swollen feet into rundown scuffs and donned a rumpled housecoat, not unlike the old blue rag I loved for its comfort but hoped never to be caught wearing. The wig I'd assumed real had been removed. Traces of gray-pink scalp showed between thin strands of hair drawn tightly into a small knot at the nape of a softly wrinkled neck.

"Here," I babbled, thrusting the basket against her ample midsection before my one last scrap of courage became history. "Mylittlegirlpickedthebudsoffyourtulips. Idon'tknowwhatIcandootherthantellyouI'msorry."

Wouldn't you know! The dear lady had removed her hearing aid along with her corset. I had to slow down and repeat, not once, but twice.

When I finally got my message across, she looked stricken. "I ordered those bulbs from Holland—last fall," she said.

"Oh. Oh, dear." Even I, who had not been blessed with a green thumb, knew that first blooms are often biggest and best.

Then, as if a steel rod had been thrust alongside her aging backbone, she straightened. "My dear, think no more about it. The beauty of a blooming tulip is fleeting; a child blooms for a lifetime. Nothing must cause those precious petals to droop or to fade. Besides, she's still a baby.

"I had no children, you know—and I so enjoy observing yours. I hope you don't mind."

Mind?

After all, for the price of a basket of tulips and the cost of the mountain of courage it took to make amends, I had stood before a judge who had every right to condemn me. I had seen forgiveness in action.

Watching our youngest more closely meant I also got to see those bright Holland tulips in full bloom the next year.

Lord, my unsaved neighbor knows better how to forgive than I do. Teach me your ways—and hers! Amen.

Following a visit to the zoo, Renee was describing her first experience with live elephants to her aunt. She spoke of color and size, explained the manner in which an elephant consumes hay, and more. Having finished her story, she paused for a moment, and then said, "And then he took his snoring place and blew all over himself."

Chapter 3

Drill Bit

Your word is a lamp to my feet and a light for my path.

—Psalm 119:105, NIV

My patient and methodical husband paints rooms and other stuff like a pro. While I scan labels for "quick and easy," "dries in 10 seconds," or "one coat does it," Norm opts for every tedious step written in fine print that suggests a paint job can last both coming and going.

The one time he decided to distribute paint my way—quick and easy—ended in disaster. That little catastrophe or sitcom (however one chooses to look at it) may well have been my fault. Having placed the heavy-duty electric drill (the drill marked specifically with Norm's drool) beneath his red Christmas stocking with my own loving hands, I should neither have asked nor expected him to keep tabs on the kids while I sashayed off to a neighbor's for a home demonstration party.

Today, I cannot imagine leaving a household bouncing with preschoolers to go hear even my *best* neighbor tout cleaning products priced ridiculously beyond both supermarket prices and our budget. Not even if our moppets could be left with a loving dad blessed with diapering skills equal to my own. Then, however, an invitation to a gathering of any sort came with the promise of conversation in a language other than cherubic along with goodies baked by someone else's mom.

As I blew kisses and scurried out the door, my beloved had his new drill in one hand and was holding onto our spring-loaded toddler with the other. Directions for that fine Craftsman product he held in his hand lay on the kitchen table *in plain sight.*

Before I had reached the end of our extra-short driveway, my built-in baby sitter scanned the long list of wonders the new tool would enable him to perform and let loose of the baby. The minute his forefinger lit on "stirs paint quickly and easily," the time arrived for him to paint the crib I had asked him to redo several months before the moppet clinging to his best denims had been born.

Like a motherless puppy at the approach of a storm, Andie began to whine and strain toward where her older sisters had set up housekeeping on the porch with their dolls. Premonition? Possibly. Likely, however, only a thinking adult could have foreseen what was about to take place.

Locating the two-year-old quart of blossom pink paint I'd once selected, my partner-for-life stood our blonde one on a kitchen chair and pried open the can. Rummaging through the drill kit, he selected the attachment designed for paint stirring, locked it into the drill's nose, and plugged his tool into a nearby outlet.

"Watch Daddy," he said as he plunged the stirrer into the paint and touched the trigger.

What happened on contact could have taken the grand prize on *America's Funniest Home Videos.* Pale droplets of pink paint hit the ceiling, splattered all four walls, dripped off the stove, and speckled the cabinets. Paint soaked into clothes and did strange things to the surprised look on the face of the baby.

By the time I got home, my less-than-delighted spouse had shampooed and bathed the painted one, put his and her clothing to soak, tucked all four kids into bed, and was cleaning the last of the oil-based paint from the floor. Chagrined and weary, he slumped into a chair, retrieved what were now paint-smeared directions, and read the fine print: *Paint stirring attachment is designed for one-gallon containers only.*

While the far-flung contents of that single quart of pink paint may have seemed like a gallon during wipe-up, it was not. Starting three quarts short of the recommended amount meant suffering the consequences.

Ignoring directions is common. Sometimes we get by with it. A failure to heed biblical specs for a walk with the Lord, however, can mean chaos. That, too, tends to mess up one's offspring.

Lord, may my daily walk with you be pleasing in your sight, provide worthwhile examples to my children, and set spiritual precedents for future generations.

While demonstrating her newly acquired counting abilities to her father, Andrea counted to nineteen, skipped a number and finished triumphantly with a rousing, "21!"

"What happened to 20?" her daddy asked.

She pondered briefly, then said, "Oh, it's there on the clock someplace."

Chapter 4

Glad Rags

Why do you worry about clothes? See how the lilies of the field grow. They do not labor or spin. Yet…not even Solomon in all his splendor was dressed like one of these. If that is how God clothes the grass of the field…will he not much more clothe you…?

—Matthew 6:28-30, NIV

I suppose I could blame my best friend for what started out as an innocent shopping trip and eventually became an annual drive to collect and/or create new Easter finery at the first hint of spring.

"Come, shop with me," she said one morning after her little girl had turned two and our firstborn had taken her first tentative steps. "I want to buy my little sweetie an Easter outfit."

At the time, "Easter outfit" had not once, not even in my wildest dreams, ventured beyond the storybook section of my vocabulary. Further, I knew I could not afford to buy so much as a pair of shoestrings at the store where my friend preferred to shop. Ignoring facts, I tagged along. As soothing as it might be to my conscience to shift responsibility, my friend is in no way to blame for what happened in the baby department on the second floor of that upscale department store. For it was I, not she, who first spied the bonnet.

Anita had bonnets, of course, the prettiest of which had yet to be tied beneath her dimpled chin. But in this first-time mom's opinion, the wide-brimmed concoction on the bonnet stand before me seemed more chic. Just for fun, I lifted the bonnet from its velvety perch and the rest, as they say, is history. Never mind that half a week's groceries for three sailed into church on Easter Sunday morning via the head of a baby who could not have cared less.

One thing led to another, Easter followed Easters and, in due time, the family grew to include three little girls for whom new Easter outfits became a necessity. It was as if the plan had been written in Scripture: "Charm is illusive, and beauty soon evaporates; but let the woman be praised in the door of the church who rises before dawn and wants, then buys. She lights a lamp and sews glad rags for her children that they may worship in the splendor of her handiwork on the day of our Lord's resurrection" (Proverbs 31:32, AVLT [author's very loose translation]).

Our children, in fact, will long remember the year they shivered through Easter in sleeveless nylon dresses sewn from a gauzy yellow-on-yellow pinstripe fabric with cocoa brown trim. Likewise, none have forgotten how many years they wore those three dresses—or how long their next two sisters wore them—or the neighbor's kids.

The saga of the yellow dresses began the day Anita decided to try on her summer clothes and we discovered she'd outgrown every summery stitch in her closet. Not to worry. Summer, with its daily donning of play clothes, was coming. I would make her a new dress for Easter and it would do for Sunday school and other dress-up affairs all summer.

A questioning look came over the face of the long-term clerk in J. C. Penney's yard goods department the morning I plunked a bolt of yellow fabric onto the counter, showed her my chosen pattern, and asked for four yards. "Did you notice that this is 90-inch fabric?" she asked.

"I want the skirt to be full," I said without stopping to realize that what I had asked for was equivalent to, not four, but eight yards of the usual 45-inch fabric.

Her mouth settled into a "suit yourself" line. When I laid out the fabric at home, I saw why. To make a long story short, I cut, not one, but three look-alike dresses, sizes two, four, and six, from that fabric. Having allowed for four-inch hems, I still had scads left over!

While I'd chosen an easy pattern, cutting and sewing time multiplied by three meant that the day before Easter arrived with handwork yet to be done. Brown fabric covers had yet to be popped onto seventeen small buttons and the buttons sewed in place. Hems must be whipstitched and bias facings secured.

As I moved swiftly through the chores that make up a given Saturday in a home blessed with children, the phone rang. "Come have soup with us," my friend Darlene invited.

Darlene personified all that I pictured myself being but was not. A mother of one child, her house, like the rest of her life, seemed always in order. To invite us for a meal on Saturday night meant she had planned precisely that. Besides…

"I have a little handwork to finish on the girls' dresses. May I bring them along and stitch while we visit?" I asked.

I knew all too well why she laughed as she said, "Sure." Darlene was a good friend. She also had my number.

Following a dinner of delicious corn chowder, biscuits, and jam, I hastily helped with dishes then got on with my sewing. After visiting for a while at the table, the men opted for more comfortable chairs in front of the TV. Halfway through the last hem, I finally thought to glance at Darlene's bright kitchen clock. Chagrined to see hands pointing to 11:15, I roused my spouse (both men had fallen asleep) and together we rounded up our weary children. At home, while the rest in my household slumbered, I dyed three-dozen Easter eggs, finished hemming size two's dress and, at 1:15 A.M., dropped wearily into bed.

Easter morning dawned cool and rainy. The children refused to prefer hot cross buns over the usual Cheerios and we had to hurry them through Easter baskets. Anita's worn red school sweater did little to enhance bouffant yellow, and Jennifer could not find her best petticoat and had to make do with an old slip much too short to be worn beneath sheer. Not to be outdone,

Kristin stuffed her mouth with jellybeans and drooled purple down her front on the way to church.

Needless to say, the daddy of the trio could have won the deadhead prize for droopiest usher that morning. This mom might have done some drooping herself, except that to attempt a droop on a freshly shined pew with cranky children scrapping on lap and either side smacks of the impossible.

Sometime between the joyous singing of *He Lives* and the benediction, I awakened to words spoken in earnest by our pastor: "Let us think for a moment of those grave clothes—in disarray—forgotten—left behind—the furthermost thing, if you please, from our Master's thinking as Jesus went forth in celebration of the Resurrection he had so recently promised.

"What is it that constitutes your grave clothes this morning? What is it we need to fling aside in order to celebrate the risen Savior?"

Tired as I was, I could gladly have thrown away every shred of careful yellow stitching and tossed in three grumpy kids for good measure. That I held onto my weary self and did not, left lasting effects. All three kids, along with the two we added later, are still alive. And, according to scuttlebutt, the smallest of those yellow dresses was last seen dangling from the arm of a lady leaving a yard sale some twenty years later.

While that may be only a rumor, it is comforting to speculate on the possibility that at least some of what we do for our kids is lasting.

Lord, let the memory of those three yellow dresses forever serve as a reminder that Easter is about new life and not new clothes. Amen.

At two-and-one-half, after much licking and smearing, Anita had put together a peanut butter and jelly sandwich. Pride shone in her brown eyes as she lifted her plate, laid a chubby hand diagonally across the lopsided creation and said, "I can't use the big knife, Mommy. Will you please cut it North?"

Chapter 5

Double Whammy

And we know that in all things God works for the good of those who have been called according to his purpose.

—Romans 8:28, NIV

We had to have checked our common sense at the doctor's door the day we scheduled surgery for two on a single morning. Waiting through delicate surgery on Jennifer's four-year-old neck promised trauma enough without adding the emotional overload of a tonsillectomy for Anita. However, since progress, marked by two years of road repair had turned a twenty-minute drive to the nearest hospital into a dusty wallow of ruts and rocks, our doctor's suggestion seemed practical.

The day began smoothly enough. Miss Tonsils, being a surgical outpatient, her first-floor location made it possible for one parent to hover next to the operating room as the other wiggle-waggled tense thumbs through countless games of Simon Says with the kindergartner. Still, while trading worries on the half-hour may have lowered the count on chewed fingernails, a simple swapping of places did little to ease tension.

The steel doors marked SURGERY finally opened. As they wheeled our dimpled one into recovery, the wee hump of stillness beneath the white flannel gurney blanket seemed no bigger than when we'd first laid eyes on her. Bandages covered our child from chin to chest, and her tiny head with its wispy dark hair lay cradled in what looked like a catcher's mask.

As we gripped hands and prayed, and watched for the first faint flutter of baby eyelashes, parental concern slid center front. One glimpse of blue-gray eyes, along with reassurance that all vital signs had progressed to "satisfactory," and we scurried alongside the gurney, stepped nonchalantly into the elevator, and rumbled up to pediatrics without so much as a wave in the direction of the five-year-old.

Jennnifer reacted to surgery as if it were all in a day's play. In less time than it would have taken most grown-ups to launch into post-op moaning, she struggled sleepily to her feet and began plotting ways to escape through the old-fashioned iron crib rails surrounding her.

When a young nurse waltzed in waving a box of chocolates (courtesy of a rejected but still hoping young suitor), our white-faced moppet strained through the bars for her share. With the other two kids in the room already smearing their pallid little faces with Whitman's Sampler, what was a mother to do?

Pinching off a small taste, I tucked the bit of chocolate between lips dried and peeling from lack of water. Later I would wonder where that nurse got her training and what addled the combined three of our supposedly adult pates. Did her supervisor know that a nurse had shared sweets with some very sick children? Would my wise and wonderful mother believe that her #9 child could be so stupid?

Suddenly, all panic buttons began blaring at once. One nibble and the imprisoned one began to upchuck. Would the force of her vomiting cause bleeding? Rip out delicate stitches cosmetically designed to hide the thin scar the surgeon had promised?

The winter sky had started to darken outside the high hospital windows when the doctor finally returned to check on his small patient. Chocolate or no chocolate, vomiting could occur after almost any surgery, he assured us. Still, we had never before lived through such a scary day. We were embarrassed and we were exhausted!

Then, "By the way," the doctor said as he was leaving, "someone downstairs would like very much to see you."

Duh!

We stared at each other. Yeah. Right. When we'd left home for the hospital at 6:00 A.M., a hundred or so years ago, we'd had two kids in tow.

Flooded with shame, we began simultaneously to voice consternation.

The doctor interrupted. "Didn't the nurse tell you? Your little curly top coughed some and later developed a low-grade temp, so we opted not to do tonsils today.

Don't worry, we'd have made sure you were where you needed to be."

Downstairs, we found Anita sitting cross-legged near the foot of her bed. Fully dressed, except for her coat, both hands clutching her wee pink satchel, she sat waiting patiently to be taken home.

"It's OK," she said after we had babbled through a lame list of excuses for having left her alone for so long. "But I *was* getting a little bit lonely," she added in a small voice.

Two weeks later the tonsils came out and the two convalesced together while we recuperated from a pair of parenting experiences we'd as soon have done without.

Some time after that long day of unintentional solitary in an impersonal city hospital, our oldest began showing signs of the empathy she would one day share so well with others. And, to this day, our dimpled one can sniff out with the certainty of a bloodhound the precise flavor of chocolate that triggers bad memories.

As for two young and inexperienced parents, we know now that fair and equal are not to be confused. While we've tried our best to be fair with our children, it is impossible always to be equal. Yelling at ball games will always sound louder than quiet words of praise for a budding young pianist. And, on any given day, the kid who's hurting worst or who has the biggest problem is entitled to the lion's share of that day's parental strokes.

What's more, while that merry-go-round day in Mercy Hospital in Des Moines, Iowa included pain for all four of us, only one has a scar to show for it—and even hers is barely discernible.

Lord, I know for certain now, I may never get it all right. But I have learned this much—I know beyond doubt that I can count on you to stick around and help me gather up the pieces.

Chapter 6

Ditched

Before they call I will answer; while they are still speaking I will hear.

—Isaiah 65:24, NIV

Three shared the car with me that January day—one yeller, one baby in a car seat, and a five-year-old prophet. Born knowing the location of every item in our house, the prophet also possessed the power to predict with frightening accuracy what was going to happen if.... That she was so often right could be annoying.

"I'll need the car in the morning," I said to my partner in life on the eve of what might well be named "Mom's Big Adventure into Space."

"They're not predicting very good weather."

"I'll be OK."

Keeping the car for a day involved considerably more than a say so. In order to be at work by 7:00, the dad and breadwinner we so loved must leave the house no later than 6:30 A.M. For me, this meant rising before dark-thirty, dressing, waking the children, and grabbing enough dry toast or Cheerios to keep three kids happy for the hour-long round trip. As for Dad's breakfast, those mornings, he was on his own.

"Are you sure you want to do this? It's really nasty out," Norm said when he came back indoors after starting the car so it could warm up.

"I'll be fine."

The truth was, I'd seldom driven in bad weather; hadn't learned to drive until a couple of years after we'd gotten married. Still, my driving had improved to where I no longer felt nervous behind the wheel.

A late start meant we took the shortcut, which was almost all gravel but well maintained and a good road. Last night's freezing rain had turned the dried weeds lining the ditches into sparkling fairylands of frost and frozen droplets. Fences and power lines sagged beneath the weight of the ice and, in a dozen places along the route, giant tree limbs lay twisted and fallen. As we drove further north toward the natural gas pipeline station where Norm worked, the road that had seemed only a little icy grew worse.

"Nothing quite like an Iowa ice storm," my spouse remarked, slowing to a speed more compatible with worsening road conditions.

"Take it easy and you should be OK," he said as I slid beneath the wheel a little while later. "Those tires seem to grip the gravel pretty good."

Since speed under any conditions was not my style, I said, "Don't worry; I'll be careful," and meant it. What I didn't say was that I had no plans to retrace that graveled road route. Not with a brand new shortcut a mere four miles long leading to the highway. True, the new shortcut was also gravel, but four miles would surely prove easier than the fifteen we had just traveled.

"You're going the wrong way, Mom," said the prophet as I turned right onto a beautifully graded and nicely rounded stretch of gravel bordered by wide shallow ditches on either side.

"It's not the wrong way; it's a different way," I said, gripping the wheel, swallowing my annoyance. Unlike the road we had taken to work, the new and wider road had suddenly turned into a solid sheet of ice. Slowing to a crawl, yet moving fast enough (I hoped) to avoid stalling, I peered through the windshield. Hardly a pebble marred the smooth surface of the gravel that now lay buried beneath a thick covering of ice.

"Let's turn around," Jennifer whimpered.

"Where?" I asked through clenched teeth. What few driveways we'd passed sloped downward and were as covered with ice as the road. I drove on.

We had inched along for perhaps two miles when Anita spoke from the back seat. "Mom, I told you we were going the wrong way."

Yes, Miss Elijah, you told me.

Before I could utter a decent reply, the car suddenly developed a mind of its own. The steering wheel refused to steer and the wheels angled dangerously toward one ditch. Suddenly, for no more than an instant, we were airborne. The yeller began to yell and the prophet (a bit behind this time) predicted we were going to run in the ditch. The baby (probably the only sane person in the crowd at the moment) gurgled happily all the way over a wide sloping bank down into a bald-looking ditch equally as icy as the road we'd just left.

While the yeller yelled on and the prophet held her breath, I gently tested the brakes. Nothing. So, holding for dear life onto what had become a useless steering wheel, I did all there was left to do. I prayed, "God, help," and rode the thing out.

I don't know how far we traveled along that ditch, but quite a few power poles and three houses had slowly moved to the rear of our vision before the steering wheel suddenly decided to steer and the wheels chose that same moment to grip. Without further fanfare, we returned suddenly to the road, miraculously headed in the right direction. The yeller stopped yelling, the baby gurgled on, and the prophet noted that in spite of my going the wrong way, God took care of us.

As we crept on toward the highway where semi-trucks and other early traffic had cut wide tracks through the ice, I knew she was right. I had barely mouthed two words. The first recognized who he was; the other asked for his help, and God had heard.

There are times, I guess, when God doesn't need a whole lot of rhetoric. Once we get it into our noggins from whence comes power to change directions, he is more than willing to assist with that change.

Ditched

Lord, while I've never once, not before or since, landed in a roadside ditch, you know about all those other ditches, the ones that have nothing to do with gravel and ice. Thank you for hearing my heart's cry and for always being there to help me get back on track.

A good example does more toward the proper molding of children than do sermons—especially sermons delivered by parents.

Chapter 7

Ignored

Whoever acknowledges me before men, I will also acknowledge him before my Father in heaven. But whoever disowns me before men, I will disown him before my Father in heaven.

—Matthew 10:32–33, NIV

There have been times when I might gladly have traded my few earthly treasures for a break from kids and housework. The day our doctor diagnosed, "Appendix," and said, "It will have to come out," was not one of them.

What's more, not even the blessed advent of a child could ever influence me to consider a hospital as one of my favorite places to go. Further, our small town being short on health care facilities, the hospital to which I had to go for an appendectomy was not inside our city limits; it was twenty miles away. To make matters worse, the pictures we'd taken of our firstborn glomming a fistful of her first birthday cake had not yet been developed. What if this early talker should stumble onto a new word while I was off having my insides rearranged? Or cut tooth #5 for someone other than myself to discover? Could a still-dependent toddler survive without a mother to fill her every need? Could the mom?

Once upon a time, back when medical bills were reasonable and incisions gigantic, a hospital confinement lasting less than a week smacked of institutional incompetence. Put another way, that appendectomy, my first operation ever, seems but a distant cousin to the in-and-out, buttonhole, huge bill types of surgeries taking place today.

The pain in my gut being in total agreement with my doctor's insistence, we asked my mother to come, then reluctantly handed the baby over to a friend until Mom could get there. Two days later, lying flat on my back with a dozen black nylon butterflies holding my on-fire stomach together, I could not have cared less about the bathing and feeding of my first child. Her daddy visited faithfully each evening; Anita did not. Children were not allowed.

The minute I began to feel better, however, my ten-day confinement became a small eternity. Had Mom remembered to add water to the baby's orange juice? Was she (horrible thought) feeding her mashed potatoes and gravy as she had me? I asked the doctor for early release. He said no. On day eight, I begged my beloved to please sneak me out of the hospital and home so I could see to our little one. He shook his head.

Ignored

Day ten dawned clear and bright with the promise of home. So excited, I could barely swallow, I pushed my half-finished breakfast aside and made a face at last year's maternity dress, the dress my mother and husband had chosen with comfort in mind. Even with loose clothing, getting myself dressed took forever. Finally, my sturdier half arrived and, with a nurse hanging on to my other elbow, I gingerly lowered myself into a wheelchair and rumbled off into a maze of corridors, elevators, and wide swinging doors. Downstairs, while Norm went to bring the car around, I waited expectantly beneath a gray-striped canopy for that first joyous glimpse of my daughter.

The car stopped. My mother sat in the back seat holding Anita.

"Hi, honey," I said.

Busying herself with Mom's cameo brooch, my baby, the child I had not seen for eleven whole days, refused to look at me!

I tried again.

The curls at the nape of her neck bobbed ever so slightly.

"I missed you, sweetheart."

She buried her face in her grandmother's neck.

We were more than halfway home before she finally spoke the word that erased my held back tears—"Mommy!"

Looking back, remembering how long those days of separation had been for me, who could blame a child for assuming she'd been abandoned?

Sort of makes one wonder what goes on in the mind of the Father when we allow days and sometimes weeks to go by without spending any time with Him.

Lord, the daily joy of being with my daughter reminds me that I am your child. Perhaps you too would like to make time with me a regular part of your day. Remind me, Lord, whenever I forget.

Chapter 8

Pot Luck

A prudent man sees danger and takes refuge, but the simple keep going And suffer for it.

—Proverbs 22:3, NIV

The mercury being at 102 degrees in the shade and climbing, a kettle of hot spaghetti seemed hardly the dish to be taking to a July picnic. But with kids who'd learned from each other to turn their little sunburned noses up at regular picnic fare—coleslaw, potato salad, baked beans, and more—what was a mom to do? Besides, whenever our Sunday school class met for a family outing, our combined offspring consistently outnumbered adults. Odds were, with all those kids, my spaghetti might well become scrapings long before some of the fancier dishes taking up space on our assorted oldest tablecloths.

Having friends who knew the way to the park when we did not, we stashed a mixture of their kids and ours into the back seat of each car. The guys shoved the cooler and a container of lemonade into the trunk of our car—the car holding the oldest of our combined seven kids—and took off. While I held onto the spaghetti, my friend opened a trunk so crammed with other stuff there was no place to set it.

Not to worry.

Had a grandmother been a part of that scene, or even someone used to dealing with the law of averages, I'd have been forewarned. Since neither was present, after the trusting and, in this case, foolish manner of young moms, I set the spaghetti in the floor well behind the driver's seat, tucked two-year-old Andie back against the seat cushions, and cautioned her to stay put.

What took place less than a block from the park cannot be blamed on the fact that yesterday's infant car seats consisted of two loops of metal and a canvas sling, or that seatbelts were not standard equipment for vehicles the vintage of either our car or our friends'. I have no excuse for whatever lapse of sanity caused me to believe that a two-year-old could stay put even for an instant, let alone for three miles! This being my fourth first-hand experience with that particular age group, I can't even place blame on the sibling who pointed to a sign and hollered, "Ice cream!"

Andie scrambled to look, lost her balance, and toppled onto the lid covering the pasta. The lid tipped, plunging her wee foot into several inches of still-steaming spaghetti.

As I lunged over the seat and snatched our little one from the sibling who had somehow managed to lift her above the hot food, my friend aimed her car at the curb and jerked to a stop.

Unbuckling a soggy-looking sandal, I stripped off one pink-embroidered sock. A blister had already started to form on the top of her foot, the circle not covered by her shoe. Miraculously, the rest of her foot and ankle had hardly been burned at all.

At the park, I held onto the burned one while her dad grabbed a kit from the car and administered first aid. With the ointment barely in place, the injured one was off and running with the rest of the children. Feeling like a plateful of my own spaghetti, I let my friend answer questions while I drew a little apart to reflect on God's goodness in the face of mankind's stupidity. I rejoined the group in plenty of time to field flak from some of the guys over spaghetti they insisted bore the distinct flavor of "toe jam."

While the stepped-in spaghetti never made it onto the picnic table, and our blonde one still wears a trace of a scar from that day, things could have been a whole lot worse.

Even so, common sense is God-given and an attribute he surely intended for us to use. A little advance thinking on my part might have prevented that scar. In fact, I've since found that an occasional application of common sense helps keep both our offspring and their mother out of hot water—as well as hot spaghetti sauce.

Lord, slow me down and teach me to think. Turn my careless ways into carefully thought out plans. And, thank you again, Father, for your protection and for your healing touch.

"Mom, may I go to Mark's?"

"Not now."

"Then can I go to Jean's?"

"No, not today."

"OK then, if I can't go to Mark's and I can't go to Jean's, I get a cracker.

(Long pause)

"Half a cracker?"

Chapter 9

Scapegoat

As a dead fly gives perfume a bad smell, so a little folly outweighs wisdom and honor.

—Ecclesiastes 10:1, NIV

The day we moved into the rambling old house, we knew Charley came with the deal. Not to worry. With a yard the size of a city block, who needed the adjoining barn or pasture? Or cared that the grizzled old renter of pasture and barn owned goats? That Charley often dropped in at mealtime and failed to recognize bedtime (both ours and his) were minor problems.

In addition to goats, Charley owned a farm having sturdy barns and a lovely old farmhouse furnished in birds-eye maple. Following the death of his wife, for reasons known only to himself, Charley leased both house and farmland to friends and moved into the basement.

Using an old buffalo robe for a cover, he slept on a bare mattress on the floor and cooked piecemeal on a single-burner hotplate. Charley shaved once a week, changed tattered garments long after they gave out, and bathed no less often than his Billy goats. Somehow, it came as no surprise when this lonely old man began to think of us as family.

Having grown up on a farm, I could deal with it that first cold February when Charley tenderly carried a newborn kid from his barn to our basement and placed it in a box made cozy with rags beside our coal furnace. As a child, the space in back of our old-fashioned cook stove had often served as nursery for early lambs. I even knew to warm milk and finger-dribble it between the half-frozen lips of the steady stream of animal babies that might never have made it had Charley not brought them into our house to thaw.

The goats and I got along fine in fact until Charley's favorite, Isobel, picked the coldest night of the year to present him with twins. Much too early the next morning, Charley came in wearing a grin the size of a banana.

"Methinks three pretty little kittens may want to don mittens and come to the barn with Charley," he said.

I explained that Kristin (Charley's favorite next to Isobel) had a nasty cold and couldn't go out. Bundling the older girls into boots and warm snow gear, I wrapped scarves over their faces and watched from the kitchen window as they struggled to follow Charley through the snowdrifts between our house and the barn.

I had gotten dressed and was about to don shoes and socks when the back door burst open and the girls tumbled in followed by Charley. In one hand, Charley carried a brown gunnysack bulging with two bleating kids. With the other, he grasped the silken scruff attached to the neck of a totally frightened Isobel.

"If my little darlin' can't go to Isobel's babes, then there's nothing to be done but to bring Isobel's babes to see my darlin'," Charley explained in the St. Nicholas tone that never failed to bring our toddler running.

While Isobel stared in wide-eyed terror, Charley lifted the twins from the bag onto my clean kitchen floor for Kris to admire.

The displacement of her children proved too much for poor Isobel. Lowering her head, she positioned herself to charge. Wet hooves being no match for high-shine vinyl, she slid onto her rump and crashed into the front of the stove.

Scrambling to her feet, she then did what all frightened animals are prone to do when cornered. As little round goat droppings peppered across the floor and landed near the feet of my children, I lost my cool.

"Charley! Get that stupid animal out of my house. Now!" I hollered.

Squatting, lifting the runny-nosed one onto a knee eye level with his goat babies, Charley winked at Kris and said, "Methinks your mamma is a mite put out. But what could a gentleman do? We couldn't have Isobel out there in the cold thinking we'd run off with her babes, now could we?"

My once-clean house had started to reek of Isobel and I could no longer stand the sight of Charley.

"Out," I commanded, pointing Charley to the door. Forgetting my shoeless feet, I barely missed stepping on one of Isobel's unwelcome deposits.

"Methinks the lady needs shoes," Charley said, neatly side-stepping my command. "What size would she be wearing?"

"The exact right size for raising a bump on the head of an old goat herder if he doesn't get those animals out of this house this minute," I warned.

After a blast of frigid air announced that Charley had finally gotten the message, I scrubbed the kids along with both stove and floor and sprayed all but the kids with Lysol.

Early the next morning, Charley rapped lightly before sticking his grizzled face against my clean kitchen door pane as if nothing had changed. Still simmering, I said a weary, "Come in," and kept on jabbing at a skillet already scrubbed clean.

A bag rustled and a pair of black patent pumps appeared on the counter.

"The gentleman noticed a shoe sale on his way to the auction," Charley said in a contrite voice. "They're not kid leather, but perhaps they can help the lady to forget Isobel's bad manners."

I didn't have to read the name on both bag and box to know the shoes were expensive. They were also the right size and the closest Charley ever came to an apology.

I forgave him, of course and, while Charley remained unkempt and a nuisance, he never again turned goats loose in my kitchen. Still, since he'd blamed the affair on Isobel, for as long as we lived in that house, I never got over feeling a little nervous around birthing time until after every kid had been turned out to pasture.

I know now I should have spent more time explaining to Charley about the cure for loneliness to be found in Jesus. He, for sure, needed to know that, because Jesus took sin's rap once and for all, the need for a scapegoat (Leviticus 16:3-28) no longer exists.

That ought also to have been good news for poor Isobel.

Thank you Father for Jesus. Help me to be bold to share my faith in you with at least some of the Charleys who happen across my path.

"Run quick. Look outside," I said to four-year-old Andrea one early December morning.

"Well, what do you know," she said after a moment. "It snowed just enough to get the yard clean."

Chapter 10

Stitch Glitch

Pride goes before destruction, a haughty spirit before a fall.

—Proverbs 16:18, NIV

The very spring this mom decided Anita needed a lightweight coat, a color her sister Kris referred to as "yucky green" appeared in clothing store windows throughout the Northwest. *Chartreuse!* The very word intrigued me, as did a mental picture of our brown-eyed, freckled nose, honey blonde sweetheart clad in the latest color fashion. Never mind that a drove of little girls concurred with Kris.

The brown-eyed one, however, squealed with delight the day I dumped fabric for the dream coat from bag to kitchen table and invited her to "Come look."

"The coat lining will match the dress," I said, showing her a soft piece of pale fabric imprinted with tiny baskets of brown flowers with chartreuse leaves.

Thankful for the few tailoring skills a longsuffering college instructor had drilled into my happy-go-lucky head, I plunged into a project a seamstress with less chutzpah would have called difficult. Somehow, I managed to slow my slap-bang self down, follow directions to the letter, and make the project work.

Eventually (it's a good thing I started early), both coat and dress got finished, pressed, and hung on my best padded hanger. When Sunday finally came, and Anita donned the pale yellow straw left over from last Easter, there was not a shred of doubt. Our pretty little second grader would wow the whole church and be the envy of every other girl, including those who hated chartreuse. Whether or not that happened, I will never know. The minute we slowed to a stop in the church parking lot, she ran off to Sunday school. Children's church being next, we never saw her again until after church when she showed up long enough to beg to go home for the day with a friend.

In reply to my first question, her friend Melanie, two years older and one foot taller, said, "She can wear some of my outgrown clothes to play in."

At church that evening, we saw neither Anita nor her outfit until after we had sung a half-dozen songs and the pastor announced that, "Our boys and girls have agreed to sing for us. Come right on up here, children."

I stared in disbelief from our fifth row pew as the one given permission to spend the day with a friend walked proudly across the platform in full view of that whole church wearing a plaid gingham dress that might, by a stretch of the imagination, have fit me! Close on her heels, crammed into our daughter's new outfit and looking no less than ridiculous, came Melanie! To borrow an expression from my mother, with chartreuse sleeves stuck midway between wrist and elbow, and both dress and coat hemlines riding high on her thighs, overgrown, upstart Melanie looked as if she were "about to jump over herself."

To keep from choking on my own consternation, I glanced once more at Anita who looked happy as a proverbial clam with plaid shoulders dangling nearly to her elbows and a hemline only slightly above the floor. The worst, however, was yet to come.

After finishing their song, the children filed from the platform and, as Melanie's back came into view, I gasped. *She's ripped one sleeve half out of that coat!* All my careful matching of notches and stitching—all my trimming and pressing—the beautiful coat was ruined. And Melanie–green-eyed, jealous Melanie–had been the one to ruin it. *Wait till church gets out*, I simmered.

Wouldn't you know that would be the very evening our music director would pick a closing song telling how folks can tell we are Christians "by our love." Then, before I'd had time to speak to the people sitting behind us, Anita bounded over to us and said, "Don't I look beautiful in blue and red plaid? I just love long dresses, don't you? Melanie's mom said we could trade, but only if it was OK with me because my dress and coat were new and Melanie's wasn't. Don't worry, we're going in the restroom and trade back." She dashed between departing church folks to rejoin her friend.

"'Beauty is in the eye of the beholder,'" I muttered to a friend whose eyes danced with laughter over what she had overheard.

My friend made a face. "I'm surprised either one of them would like chartreuse," she remarked. "Most kids don't. Mine say it's the color of puke."

Since "by our love" still rang in my ears, I refrained from saying, "Well, *I* like it."

Instead, I greeted a few folks, went meekly on home, examined what I'd assumed to be total destruction, and discovered the rip wasn't half as bad as feared. When I finally got around to mending it, I caught myself grinning every now and then over a ridiculous trade that brought delight to a pair of small girls and, for a couple of hours, kept this mom (literally) in stitches. That our daughter seemed more interested in the happiness of a friend than in pride over a new outfit is probably why she tripped so joyfully onto that platform without once falling over the hem of that long dress.

Lord, thank you for innocent children who so often show me the way. Help me to learn the difference between satisfaction over a job well done and the kind of pride that provokes quarrels and leads to destruction.

Chapter 11

Lighten Up!

A gentle answer turns away wrath, but a harsh word stirs up anger.

—Proverbs 15:1, NIV

Never having had a whole lot of experience with nature's turbulence other than our usual thunder and lightning, in my vocabulary, the term *eye of the storm* belonged exclusively to our TV weatherman. It did at least until the morning Liz attacked our front doorbell with the combined furies of hurricanes, holocaust, and hullabaloo.

Waving a pink zippered pouch before my startled nose, our until then compatible neighbor babbled and gestured and breathed unholy fire until I finally deciphered her message: Jennifer, our current four-year-old (the one who at eleven months had attempted to diaper herself) had shown Liz's preschool moppet how to bring instant fire to the business end of a match.

Don't ask me how Precocious came by such sophisticated knowledge. Our one box of matches had not been out of its tin on the top cupboard shelf since we'd moved into the other half of the duplex occupied by the now-livid Liz and her family of three.

Ripping open the pink pouch, Liz extracted an unbroken pack of Lucky Strike cigarettes and a matchbook advertising Trail's End Saloon. "Bobbi looked so cute," she mourned.

Since Liz had been kind enough never to smoke in my house, I'd considered her unhealthy habit none of my business. Still, "You mean you allow Bobbi to carry cigarettes? And matches?" I blurted.

"Why is that any different from your kids playing dress up?" Liz countered.

Disturbed over what seemed to me a peculiar approach to child rearing, I said, "Bu—tobacco is—uh—matches are dangerous. She could get burned!"

"Not if your stupid little darling had stayed out of it," Liz shot back.

Tempted to retort that if our child were so stupid, how come she'd figured out how to light a match when Liz's child, whose parents lit cigarettes from dawn until who knows when had not, I breathed a prayer and calmed down.

"Liz, I'm sorry," I said. "Bobbi didn't get burned, did she?"

"No. But her fun's ruined. She hung onto her little pack of smokes like some kids carry dolls. It was her way of playing Mommy. Having to hide all the matches is going to be a nuisance."

Out of deference to our being "religious," Liz almost always apologized whenever she fell back on words from what she called her blue-striped vocabulary. Worked up like she was, if she saw stripes at all that morning, they surely must have been red ones.

The insulated wall separating Liz's side of the duplex was necessary. Allowing a wall of contention to divide us as neighbors was not.

"I hope you'll forgive me for not watching the children more closely," I said, after handing over to the Lord several retorts that were too big to swallow. "I'll have a talk with Little Miss Firebug."

My soft answer worked. Liz returned the smile only God could have pasted across my scowling face. "Don't be too hard on her; she's only four," she said.

No spectacular turnaround followed Liz's about-face. Still, come August, she let Bobbi go with our kids to Vacation Bible School for the first time (Bobbi went; the pink pouch stayed home).

Further, Liz's continuing neighborliness confirmed that the price of peace is sometimes being in the wrong even when you jolly well know you are not.

Oh, Lord, keep a hand over my mouth and a close watch over those quick retorts that sometimes fly like angry hornets into my thought life.

Beginning with the first hymn, Kristin's church behavior that morning had been considerably less than acceptable even for a toddler. Finally, her exasperated father carried her from the sanctuary to a distant corner of the foyer and told her to stop tantalizing her older sister. To emphasize, he then administered a single swat to her diaper-padded bottom.

She sniffled quietly against her father's shoulder as they returned to the sanctuary and, as they reached the end of our pew, straightened, looked at me, and tattled aloud, "H-he hit me!"

Could be the ensuing laughter was what brought a hasty end to a sermon that seemed a little dry in the first place.

Chapter 12

Hippocratic Hope

Always be prepared to give an answer to everyone who asks you to give the reason for the hope that you have.
—1 Peter 3:15, NIV

The sage green station wagon sitting in the shade of the carport, its doors gaping, had been ours (in tandem with my spouse's company credit union) for two whole weeks. Even before we signed papers, we knew that this marvel of Ford Motor Company design would provide perfect transportation for the family vacation scheduled to begin the minute our breadwinner arrived home from work at 4:30. We would fold its seats down, throw in a pad, assign a corner to each child, and stash luggage in a pod latched onto the top of the new-to-us vehicle.

Occupied with stuffing more into said luggage than it had been designed to contain, I gave scant attention when our second grader remarked on her way to the carport, "You're busy, aren't you?"

Five minutes past the birth of our first child, I knew instinctively that there was more to "busy" than Ma Bell had in mind when she attached the word to a telephone signal. For me, and a billion other mothers, busy was a way of life. On this particular day, however, "busy" seemed hardly adequate for a condition that might better be described as pushed, shoved, frenzied, and crammed.

"I can get the car ready," Jennifer volunteered as I slapped a pile of little girl shorts into a gaping suitcase and answered with a distracted "Mmm," which she interpreted to mean "Please, do." Minus the help of her two-year-old sibling, she might have managed.

As I scrambled on top of the suitcase in a last-ditch attempt to force its latches to meet, the happy sounds of the children turned into frightened screams, catapulting the mom of the brood from luggage to carport in the proverbial nothing flat.

Andie had been warned, three voices screeched in unison.

One glance at the dangling tip of a tiny finger and I knew she had not moved quickly enough to escape the crashing of station wagon seats. I knew, too, that the finger was going to need stitches. The trouble was, the (then) six of us had remained amazingly healthy following our last recent move and we had neglected to sign on with a doctor.

While Anita ran for the telephone directory, Jennifer rallied with an offer to "go tell Cindy's daddy because

Cindy's daddy is a doctor and Cindy's daddy's doctor office is in his house." She knew Cindy's daddy was home because she could see Cindy's daddy's car in the driveway at the end of our street.

Thrusting the injured one into the arms of our oldest, I told Miss Second Grader to stay put, grabbed the directory, and dialed the number assigned to Cindy's daddy's house.

While the clock ticked on and blood dripped over the child I'd intended to take on vacation and the floor I'd intended to leave clean, I listened with dismay to Cindy's daddy's wife explain that she was sorry; the doctor did not have time to involve himself with neighborhood first aid.

As she launched into a spiel having to do with the importance of the doctor's clientele, I interrupted, "Please, may I speak with the doctor?"

While waiting, I remembered last week's birthday party and almost hung up. Although the girls walked arm-in-arm to school and romped daily through each other's houses, Cindy had matter-of-factly explained to Jennifer, "I can't invite you because your mom and dad are not our friends."

Cindy's daddy barely heard me out before announcing that, as a busy surgeon, he seldom dealt with cuts and bruises. He also had an appointment at the golf course in less than an hour.

So much for the Hippocratic (hypocritical?) oath! Later I would learn that the major portion of Cindy's daddy's importance resided in the minds of him and his wife and that his surgery schedule consisted mostly of the wholesale tonsillectomies taking place at the time.

Still, he did us a favor. In reply to my shrill insistence, he gave me the name and location of a doctor nearby, "A young fellow just getting a start who could probably use your business."

Wall-to-wall patients crowded the waiting room of that "young fellow just getting a start." Yet, one glance at the injured finger lying against the damp washcloth I held in my hand and we were immediately ushered into a sparkling clean room. The young doctor promptly and calmly cleaned, stitched, and dressed the wee finger as if our two-year-old were the most important person in his day.

As we drove home in our station wagon, I explained to the kids that there was no way now that we could begin our vacation on schedule. "However," I added, "we are four balloons, four cherry-flavored lollipops and one fine doctor richer, aren't we?" Whether or not that young man "could use our business," he was going to get it for a long as we lived in that place.

As for Cindy's daddy, I suppose I shouldn't be too hard on him. While my medical know-how is limited to doling out ready-made bandages and doctoring stubbed toes, I happen to hold in my heart the only sure cure for his brand of self-centeredness and I never once bothered to share Jesus with him.

Lord, few seem to want to be bothered with hearing about Jesus, including some of my neighbors. Please lead me to those who have open hearts and are willing to allow me to tell them about my best Friend.

Shortly after she began first grade, the feisty one developed a crush on the school principal. While she talked about him daily, and giggled whenever she spoke his name, her infatuation was obviously no more than a game. We knew this for sure the day she came home from school and, in exasperated tones, confided, "He keeps calling me Honey. I finally had to tell him my real name!"

Chapter 13

Trail of Tires

If I go up to the heavens, you are there; if I make my bed in the depths, you are there. If I rise on the wings of the dawn, if I settle on the far side of the sea, even there your hand will guide me, your right hand will hold me fast.

—Psalm 139:8-10, NIV

The first ten miles of our move from Midwest to Northwest proved beyond the shadow of an Iowa cornfield that a long distance move is best left to pros. What we told our young and idealistic selves was that this was a career change. In reality, translated into grueling and get-rid-of-stuff words, it meant that none of those big vans came around at company expense the day we packed our worldly goods into a trailer devoid of springs and headed off on our biggest adventure ever.

Somewhere along the dull ribbon of unbending and seemingly endless Nebraska highway, on a day when you could have boiled coffee on the pavement, the first tire blew.

Hot and tired as we were, we could relax. Norm (the man for whom we were making this move) had mounted a spare tire back in Illinois before our journey began. One quick tire change and we would be on our way. That might well have happened had the one responsible for spreading both peanut butter and good cheer remained upright and able to continue with helping to engineer a smooth move. But the body doubled over and barfing beside the road belonged neither to the one changing tires nor to the four kids chasing along the dusty ditch scaring the "tobacco juice" out of a horde of winged grasshoppers.

Whether my nauseous illness got its start through lurking germs, lack of air conditioning, or one too many bologna sandwiches, remains a mystery. Whatever the cause, more repeats of that "barf 'n' tire stop" than I care to remember slowed progress for 401 miles across Wyoming and well into Idaho.

While the wind blew and I retched, my patient partner put still another spare together beneath the blue skies too far west of Cheyenne and the green grass of Wyoming for either town or turf to be of any use. Remembering the two-year-old among the kids searching for fossils along a highway where traffic seldom happened but was dangerously fast, I lifted my face from between my knees and saw two strangers walk over the hill looming before us.

Angels? Good. We could use a couple.

In case they were not, I struggled to my feet, located a tire tool, and shooed the kids inside the station wagon. Gripping the tool with both hands, I wobbled to where Norm knelt tightening lug nuts, propped my shaky knees against the back bumper, and sized up the men who were now less than a buffalo wallow away.

Cowboys come with boots, and ranchers seldom walk highways. A closer look and the two pale, sunburned men no longer fit into my slot marked angels. Not with tobacco juice dribbling down unshaven chins onto twin gray shirts and trousers that looked as if they'd been slept in.

The men stopped, chewed, spat, and offered to help.

"Thanks, but no; I'm finished," Norm said, wiping sweat from his face, coolly letting down the jack while keeping a close eye on the rest of the tools.

No music has ever been so sweet as the popping into place of that battered old hubcap accompanied by the receding crunch of four nondescript clodhoppers.

"D-e-p-a-c-s-e s-t-c-i-v-n-o-c?" I asked, spelling backwards so not even our third grader could guess as we piled back into the car and drove off.

My tire specialist shrugged.

While we will never know, an angel, I think, would have noticed my discomfort and offered sympathy. Those two—without so much as a glance in my ailing direction—had simply stood beside the road splattering their tobacco juice over the fauna and fossils characterizing that wide arid ditch.

Near Sinclair, Wyoming, our tire predicament dropped from awful to acute. Sinclair did not do tires. What's more, no kind angel had tinkered that high country thermostat onto a temperature more compatible with our lack of air conditioning. As the man in the sweat-soaked shirt drove off toward Rawlins and what had better be someone who did tires, the girls and I headed for some puny patches of shade offered by Sinclair's one small park. While the kids shuffled through parched grass, took turns with two swings, and drank our water jug dry, I sat with my back against a scrawny tree and pondered resourcefulness as applied to our eldest should I die on the spot.

An hour passed; then two; three, and nearly four. I reminded myself that my beloved had racked up enough "second miles" in the last few days to do for a lifetime. Who could blame him if he'd chosen to take the easy way out, wheeled through Rawlins, and driven off into the sunset?

Jennifer plunked her sweaty little body onto the hard sandy soil beside me. Perspiration dropped from her dark hairline and dripped off my elbow as she leaned for a while against my arm.

She heaved a giant sigh. "Mom, does God know we're in Wyoming?"

I find it best not to dwell on what my reply might have been had her father not driven back into our lives along about then.

"Sure, he does," I said with a smile, and added under my breath, *"and—finally—so does your father."*

The temperature had climbed to 108 degrees the day we stopped somewhere in southern Idaho to replace still one more tire. Other than that, we finally made it to our Washington State destination without further mishap.

For some time now, we've had reason to travel that same route at least once a year. I know this sounds crazy after all these years, but I would declare the sagebrush grows especially lush over those roadside places where this author had to holler "Stop! Now!" as we took that first long journey along a lonely highway toward a job that wasn't all that great after we got there.

Lord, you not only knew we were there, you never once forgot we were there! Thanks!

Chapter 14

Thorn Theology

If we confess our sins, he is faithful and just and will forgive us our sins and purify us from all unrighteousness."

—1 John 1:9, NIV

The day God created trees, he surely never intended for the honey locust ever to be planted in yards marked out by unsuspecting young parents for the growing of children. Why am I so sure? Because those sweet-smelling blossoms that so perfume the air and stir up dormant allergies are deceiving. Hidden beneath lacy layers of the shade that feels so good to perspiring bodies on a hot summer day are thorns. Not occasional thorns, but big thorns, little thorns, and every other size thorn only an expert could possibly imagine—thorns to plague the unsuspecting steps of every child who ever loved the freedom of going barefoot in summer.

A discussion on tree species was not on the agenda the day we plunked down every dime of our squeezed-nickel savings and signed papers saying we were now the proud owners of a house we'd agreed in advance was already too small for our growing family. Buying that first house was a start, however, and all we could afford at the time. To quibble over shared rooms or landscaping (in this case, a mature honey locust obviously planted to age along with the house) seemed out of the question.

When I first discovered just how generously the old tree scattered its thorns, I issued an ultimatum: "If you kids want to go barefoot, you're going to have to play in the back yard. If you want to play in the front yard, wear shoes."

For a time, repeated warnings and a few sharp encounters seemed to solve the problem. But what child in her right mind wants to stop for shoes on a hot day in July in the middle of a squirt gun fight?

The organized one eventually came up with what seemed a workable plan. They all trooped into the house, collected their flip-flops, and placed them in a neat row beside the west back corner of the house. Even a child in flight, they reasoned, could pause long enough to slide bare toes onto a single rubber strap, especially since the one in pursuit must pause and do likewise. A mother of many soon learns never to ask questions like, "So what goes on if someone happens to run around the *east* side?" Sensible questions are not popular with kids carrying out a plan of their own—especially not a plan that worked well for a time.

Months later—more than half a year in fact—Kris hopped into the kitchen one Saturday in May and announced, "Mom, I've got this weird bump on the bottom of my foot. It's kind of whitish."

Shoe in hand, she waited patiently while I washed and wiped my hands.

"Does it hurt?" I asked.

"Not unless it pokes."

"What do you mean 'pokes'?"

"It kind of stabs. That hasn't happened for a long time. But the spot keeps getting bigger and now there's this blackish dot."

"You probably have something in it. I'll get a needle."

Her grin faded. "Do you have to?" she asked as I dipped the needle in rubbing alcohol and lifted her pudgy foot onto my lap.

This was our tomboy, the kid who preferred barefoot over any style of footgear one could offer. Her maternal grandfather likely would have called the toughened skin on the ball of her foot "whang leather." Locating a larger needle, I probed harder.

The gunk that accompanied a half-inch honey locust thorn in response to my probing might have filled a small thimble. To prevent further infection, I cleansed and swabbed the wound with antiseptic and silently thanked God and our doctor for a recently administered tetanus shot given for another reason. The foot healed quickly and left no trace of a scar.

Still, as moms are prone to do, I had to ask, "Why on earth did you wait so long to show me? Did you think it would just go away? Surely having a thorn in your foot all winter must have hurt!"

She mumbled something and when I asked her to please speak up, she said, "You said not to play in the front yard in our bare feet and I guess I did it anyhow. I guess sin always finds you out, huh, Mom?"

At least she could recall Scripture even if she couldn't remember to put on her shoes. "Sin also jabs at the conscience. If left to fester, it can cause all kinds of problems," I reminded.

The analogy ends here, for sin left to fester almost always leaves a scar. Strange, isn't it, how long we sometimes hang onto our thorns and our sins when Mom or God would gladly do whatever it takes to relieve us of either one?

Lord, if sin festers even in the smallest corner of my heart, please cleanse it away and inoculate me with your Holy Spirit against future infections.

Chapter 15

Frozen Assets

Even a child is known by his actions, by whether his conduct is pure and right.

—Proverbs 20:11, NIV

"I'm going to help Jimmy gather icicles," the middle one announced one bright morning following a winter storm. "Is it OK if we use those apple boxes out in the shed?"

Squeezing tepid water from a soapy white washcloth, I wiped lint from our current baby's rosy neck folds and murmured a distracted, "If you put them back."

Two hours later, our disgruntled icicle picker slammed into the kitchen and peeled off a wet scarf.

"Nobody wants to buy any icicles," she complained, dropping snow-crusted mittens onto the register to dry. "We stopped at every house and all the neighbors were home and they still didn't buy any icicles—not even for three cents!"

With that single closing statement, she had gained my full and indignant attention. "You have been going up and down this street, bothering our neighbors, trying to sell icicles?"

"We didn't need the apple boxes. All the icicles that didn't already break fit in the wagon."

Kris, the budding entrepreneur standing wide-eyed before me letting snow melt from her fur-lined boots onto my clean floor, was not in first but in fourth grade! And even if icicle peddling had been an all right thing to do, considering present weather conditions, our neighbors all had plenty of icicles of their own.

"What in the name of good sense made you think anyone would want to buy icicles?" I demanded.

Ignoring my question, she babbled on, "Jimmy says colored icicles will sell better. We're going to put some in their freezer and some in our freezer and save them for next summer. After everyone's icicles have melted, we can paint ours and sell them."

"No."

She blinked.

"Even if the freezer were empty, which it is not, you are not storing icicles, colored or uncolored. Not now; not next summer."

"Why not?"

Tipping her chin, demanding eye contact, I said, "I cannot believe a big girl like you would try to sell anybody nothing for something when it is not anything."

Seeing her brown eyes dance, I smiled and we burst into laughter over what I had just said.

After our giggling had subsided, I reminded Miss Icicle Saleslady that Jimmy was younger and gifted with uncommon imagination. I said that imagination is one of the fabulous fringe benefits more generously supplied by God to some than to others. I suggested that Jimmy would probably grow up to write fiction or become an inventor.

"You," I said, "are old enough to know better."

The apple boxes remained in the shed and the last of the icicles finally dripped from the wagon during a February thaw.

Some time later, as we read aloud from a well-worn Bible story book, we came to the story of Amos, the prophet who lashed out at people for boosting prices and weighing with dishonest scales (Amos 8:1–6).

"Know what—I'll bet Amos tried to sell icicles when he was a kid. If they had icicles in Bible days, he probably charged *four* cents," our middle one said. She then speculated, "Probably nobody bought any, so when he grew up, he already knew it was wrong, so he could tell other people to be fair. Cheating just doesn't work, does it, Mom?"

I hated to tell her, but neither does painting icicles.

Lord, the way we treat our neighbors is probably going to be the way our children will one day treat theirs. To always be fair is a tall order, so please help us as we strive to model Jesus in still another area of our lives.

"Mommy, where do kisses go when you're done with them?"

If she had asked me today instead of back then, I would say, "God takes them with joy and stores them in hearts."

Chapter 16

While Visions of Sewing Pins Danced in My Head

Train a child in the way he should go, and when he is old he will not turn from it.

—Proverbs 22:6, NIV

A principal with principles, Mrs. Merritt ought to have been cloned. Place a buxom Merritt copy in a zillion elementary schools, allow time for her influence to spiral down, and from sitcom to Supreme Court, things would change.

Mrs. Merritt in charge meant that the 400 or so students attending her school toed a mark she had indelibly drawn. So did their parents. Mothers baked, read, room-mothered, and herded kids through field trips at the drop of a multi-colored notice. Fathers considered it prudent to get involved and to show up alongside Mom for parent-teacher conferences. Believe me, a good old Merritt going over on the subject of caring about kids was not a lecture a parent wanted to hear more than once!

That Mrs. Merritt considered each child to be more than a blur in the crowd became apparent soon after we'd moved to that community. The day I scurried into her office to enroll our five-year-old in first grade, she ran our blonde one through a list of readiness hoops and shook her head.

"Chronologically, perhaps; social and other skills, emphatically no. Let her play for another year and you'll never be sorry," she advised, and she was right.

My initiation into Mrs. Merritt's planned parent participation happened that same first year on a Saturday night exactly two working days before school dismissed for Christmas break.

"Oops, I forgot," the complacent one said after baths had been taken and we were settled on her bed with two library favorites and one Bible story book.

Pulling a crumpled envelope from between the tattered pages of *Harold and the Purple Crayon*, Kris informed me, "Mrs. Merritt said 'Don't forget; give this to you right away.'"

I glanced at my watch and tucked the envelope into my skirt pocket. "OK, but first let's read," I said.

Two books, one Bible story, and four prayers, kisses and trips to the bathroom later, I finally collapsed into my favorite chair and opened the envelope.

Dear parents, the letter began. *Your 3 children are an important part of our learning team here at Wide Hollow School. Because they are new students here, and because we believe it beneficial for other students as well as the community to get to know them, we have given your child/children a prominent role in our annual Christmas program.*

Names of new students, it seemed, had been unintentionally left off a list. To make up for the error, Mrs. Merritt now wished to give each of those children the special attention she believed due new students. She then apologized for any inconvenience caused by her failure to explain school policy concerning costumes early on. In reality, had it not been left for so long between the pages of *Harold and the Purple Crayon*, the letter had been sent in plenty of time.

Skimming on to page 2, I yelped. Hearing me, the tucked ones bolted from their beds and stood, wide-eyed, before me. I sent them back to bed. It is never good for children to witness even imagined mayhem.

Alone once more, my thoughts spun as I realized I had better believe and believe mighty quickly what I had just read. A desperate glance at the clock on top of the bookshelf told me more than I wanted to know. At 9:27, stores had of course closed and tomorrow was Sunday. How in the wildest of high energy spurts was one overworked and underpaid mother going to outfit Anita as Ma Santa, create one candy cane clown suit, and come up with a nurse doll uniform by 7:30 P.M., program time, Tuesday?

On Sunday, wishing I could believe in the magic of Harold's purple crayon, I borrowed one red circle skirt and a pair of high boots from a friend.

Monday morning, ignoring chores, I blitzed through yard goods, slung patterns, bolts and notions onto a counter before a yawning clerk and departed my favorite fabric store in record time. Having sold our ailing sewing machine before we moved to someone I pray had more patience than I, I wheeled into a friend's driveway on the way home and swapped one preschooler (still in pajamas and clinging to her breakfast toast) for a day with my friend's smooth-running portable.

The chaotic whirl of pins and patterns, failures and fittings that took place over the next two days is best left to the imagination. Let it suffice to say that one last fluff of quilt batting got basted to the hem of the red skirt Tuesday evening on our way to the gymnasium. And that a frisky brown reindeer managed to yank one poorly stitched sash off a nurse outfit before one of a dozen blue-and-white clad nurse dolls could respond to her cue. Through some miracle wrought by haphazard stitching, elastic bands around each ankle kept the crotch of a red-and-white striped clown suit from quite touching the floor.

After warbling on pitch and without a hitch through her solo, Ma Santa spent most of the next day de-fluffing and returning her costume to its owner. I unpinned the white apron, sewed the yanked sash firmly into place, and the nurse outfit became Jennifer's favorite school dress.

As for the clown suit, that ingenious creation fit not only a full range of sizes, but attended assorted costume parties, outlived Mrs. Merritt and, last I knew, was still making the rounds among the grandkids.

Mrs. Merritt was but one among many who helped us to bring up our children in the way they should go.

The clown suit, I think, adds tangible proof to those fluffy yellow Easter dresses that at least some of what we do for our children is lasting.

Lord, thank you for the many Christians who serve daily in our schools, people who, like Mrs. Merritt, not only care for our children but strive each day to model Jesus in their classrooms.

Having fallen from the school playground monkey bars at recess, Anita described to us the feat she had dared to attempt before losing her grip. Lacking words to explain what it felt like to have the wind knocked out of her, our kindergartner paused briefly then said, "All of a sudden, I wasn't even there."

Chapter 17

Skyline

Guard the good deposit that was entrusted to you—guard it with the help of the Holy Spirit who lives in us.

—2 Timothy 1:14, NIV

Our decision to provide each of our five children with a stay-at-home mom involved sacrifice. While our bank balance, like our aging vehicle's gas tank meant we lived on fumes for more years than a person of affluence would care to believe, we survived on love and careful spending. Stuff was what other people bought. Extras, like hiring a babysitter, happened once a year, usually on our anniversary. To pay a babysitter for any other reason required major planning.

Home being where I spent the major part of my time, I tried a couple of times to add to the family coffer by babysitting. While the "one might as well watch five as four" principle worked well for others, finding unhappy little ones on my doorstep at 6:00 A.M. so interrupted my peace of mind and the nursing and rearing of our own children, I soon opted out.

Still, while looking after the offspring of friends or neighbors increased household decibels and emptied the cookie jar, caring for children we knew (and who knew the ropes at our house) was like adding a temporary extension to our already big family. Babysitting for pay when our next-door neighbor got called to work for a short time was like that. Accustomed to running in and out of our homes as often as did dishwater, her two older children adapted with great gusto to the arrangement. Even the baby seemed content.

Childcare of any sort, however, is not for sissies.

Being at the rapid-crawl stage, Joey could hardly be sent outdoors on nice days to play with the rest. Due to his remarkable talent for unloading a cupboard faster than I could wipe jellied fingerprints from a door, tending Joey often delayed my intention to keep abreast of what the rest were up to.

The morning Diamond Oil delivered our winter's supply of furnace fuel, Joey's brother and sister, along with our youngest, were all in plain sight. Like birds on a power line, their eyes on the red truck backing into our long driveway, the three teetered beneath the kitchen window near the edge of the sidewalk. As the truck stopped beside the garage, I watched the children run to view a procedure I now knew by heart.

The deliveryman, clad in a red plaid shirt and a gray jacket with oil stains on the front, would first lift into place a short ladder kept hanging on the back of the garage for his use. The ladder barely reached the oil drum that sat a hair below the garage eaves on a scaffold-like platform. Standing on the top rung of the ladder, he would remove the barrel's cap, dismount, uncoil a section of hose, drape it over a broad shoulder and again mount the ladder. The children would watch until the last drop of oil had been pumped into the tank and the cap replaced.

Following a short wait, I opened the back door and heard him tell the children to go over on the grass and stay there until after he had driven the truck out onto the street. Since he had the situation well in hand, I swooped a now fussy Joey into the rocker, read him a story, and lowered him into his playpen for a morning nap. When I returned to the kitchen, all was quiet in the back yard—too quiet.

After quickly scanning our tiny front yard, which was close to the street and not a safe place for small children to play, I dashed back through the house, opened the door to an empty back yard and began a losing battle with panic. Hearing an angelic babbling that appeared to come from thin air, I looked up. My heart plunged from full-scale alarm to panic.

Silhouetted against a blue September sky, bobbing and chattering along the top of our single car garage, were the missing three small heads for which I was responsible. A row of grubby fingers clinging to a gray-shingled ridge pole was all, in my current state of shock, that kept those babies from plunging straight off that roof into eternity!

While my first impulse was to yell for them to get their naughty little selves off that roof this minute, instinct warned me to proceed with caution. Willing a smile to my fear-stiffened face, I quietly climbed the ladder the deliveryman had neglected to return to its place. Calling each by name, I coaxed the children one at a time to let go of the ridgepole and slide backwards down the gently sloping roof to where I could reach them and help them down the ladder.

"Hours" later, after the three were safe on the ground and the ladder back on its usual hooks, my knees still trembled with fright—a feeling that would forever after surface at the sight of a child near danger.

As our children grew older, dangers for all five loomed larger. Far too often, quiet coaxing fell on deaf ears. Looking back, recalling how I sometimes had to fuss and scold, I'm glad the Holy Spirit never raises his voice. In fact, if the rearing of our children had been left entirely to this clay-footed mom, at least five high-minded kids could have crashed before their grubby little sneakers located a toehold and touched back on solid ground.

Lord, contrary to popular belief, I do not have eyes in the back of my head. Neither have I the power to be omnipresent. So, while you're keeping an eye on all the little sparrows, please help me keep an eye on my kids.

As Renee attempted to demonstrate for an older sister how well she could whistle, she repeatedly dissolved into a fit of giggles. Finally, she said, "You'll just have to wait until I can get the funny off my face."

Chapter 18

Work Shirk

Whatever you do, work at it with all your heart, as working for the Lord, not for men.

—Colossians 3:23, NIV

Self-discipline was not one of my strong points during my growing up years. If it had been, I might possibly have finished college and made some sort of mark in the world (however faint) before taking on the awesome responsibilities of wife and homemaker-mother. Could be I arrived at this conclusion after the kids came up with an innovative clean-the-playroom system that modeled my lackadaisical housekeeping habits to the proverbial "T."

Getting a start at building home equity meant getting by with less than the ideal. In the first house we were fortunate enough to own, the girls shared a bedroom that looked more like bunk space in an economy ski lodge than a boudoir for young ladies. Since quadruple bunks left scant room even for dressing, we carted most of their toys to the least used end of the basement and created what might loosely be called a playroom.

A playroom, of course, must, at times, be cleaned. The mother of the children who play therein must periodically take time to deal with discarded dress-up clothes, old school papers, and the remains of real food tea parties. Failure on the part of a mom to do so could entail broken bones or the possibility of losing a moppet beneath the rubble. This playroom, however, was out of sight and the girls big enough to clean up their own messes. So while I baked cookies, perused the latest issue of *House Beautiful*, and dreamed up ways to avoid housework, those who plotted below had, for-who-knows-how-long, been putting my puny examples of procrastination to shame.

Unlike vacuuming, laundry for a family the size of ours can only be postponed until big and little people start running out of underwear. Spurred by early morning words from my short-on-shorts spouse, I was at the opposite end of the basement sorting clothes when I heard a voice from the playroom giving instructions.

"You work while we play," said Anita.

Good. They had found a way to take turns, to turn work into play.

Toys thumped as I sorted on.

About to start the washer, I heard Jennifer say, "OK. Now we'll play while you work."

Two voices, two commands.

I started the washer, paused to watch before going back upstairs, and was taken aback by the scene before me. While the oldest and the tallest both sat on an old rag rug reading books, and Kris played "new baby" with the plastic family living in the dollhouse, their five-year-old sister tried to push dirt into a dustpan with a broom twice her size. Since all had their backs to me, I lingered to see what this was about.

After a little while, the oldest glanced up from her book, looked at her dad's old watch that no longer ran, and said to the diligent one, "Time's up. Now you work while we play."

Huh?

While not yet in school, the one chosen to serve as Cinderella to her scheming older sisters was no dummy. She slaved quietly through one more "you work while we play" then, blue eyes wide, whirled to face the "wicked step-sisters."

"Just when?" Andrea demanded to know, "is it going to be my turn to play while you work?"

Years later, she still recalls with no little bit of rancor those times when her sisters played while she worked and how often she was made to work while they played.

Now, seeing that they had settled their own fuss with no help from me, I tiptoed quietly back upstairs and picked up the latest issue of *Good Housekeeping*, opened, then closed it, and placed it back on the coffee table. Could be the older sisters were not the only ones guilty of playing while others worked. If I hurried…It took some doing, however, to whip a neglected house into shape before my partner for life arrived home from work at 5:30.

When he asked about the grin I couldn't seem to wipe off my face, I changed the subject. Let him find out for himself about a weekend in which he would be free enough from helping with housework to read one or two of *his* magazines.

Lord, laziness and selfishness are one pair of relatives I'd rather my children not emulate. Please, if you see either of those attributes worming their unlovely way into our household, help me to recognize their profiles. Then give me the wherewithal to slam the door.

The Cowl*
By Jennifer, age 8

A mooing cow that wanted
To be an owl and hoot,
Became a cowl and then found out
That he could only MOOT.

*Published in *Humpty Dumpty, 1969*

Chapter 19

Stingray

All a man's ways seem right to him, but the Lord weighs the heart.

—Proverbs 21:2, NIV

"I'm taking this shoe off right now so I can see what's making my foot hurt," Kris announced one September afternoon as she limped across the kitchen to hand me her daily bouquet of rumpled school papers.

Scraping the last of the peach jam I'd been making into a glass dish, I asked, "How long has your foot been hurting?"

She tugged at a shoelace replete with Dalmatian puppies. "Since I put my shoe on."

I washed my sticky hands and reached for a paper bearing the familiar red-penciled 100. "You didn't look to see what might be causing your foot to hurt?"

Grunting, yanking impatiently at a stubborn knot, she glanced reproachfully at me. "I had to hurry."

"But if it hurt—oh, never mind." Multiple years of daily dealings with five kids had made plain the futility of beating one's head against juvenile absolutes, including the oft-unsolved mysteries related to the rationale of a seven-year-old.

"Mom, you don't understand. Stephanie always gets to school first, so she always gets the blue jump rope. Today, *I* got the blue jump rope," she explained with a satisfied grin.

A grubby sneaker thumped to the floor.

As she tugged at a once-white sock, I said, "Your foot hurt but you jumped rope anyhow. Wasn't that kind of silly?"

The sock dangled. "Mom! If I got the blue jump rope and didn't use it, Stephanie would tell Mrs. Beeler and then—" she paused for breath. "And then Mrs. Beeler would make me give the blue jump rope to Stephanie."

Hopping to keep her balance, she thrust a skinny foot into my lap. Gently touching a small dark protrusion on the inside of her heel, she said, "Maybe I stepped on a needle 'n' thread."

"Oh, honey, that's not a thread; it's a stinger."

As I pondered how best to remove the stinger, a bedraggled honeybee crawled from her shoe—shoes purchased with "grow room" in mind—and began preening its torn wings. So much for the notion that bees die once they've planted a stinger!

Grabbing a fly swatter, I provided a smashing end to the bee's already crowded day. Then, clasping the sturdy body of my injured child, I crooned, "Honey, I'm so sorry."

"It's not your fault, Mom."

Perhaps not. However, because the thumping of shoes tumbling in the dryer drives me bonkers, after laundering the sneakers on Saturday, I had hung them outdoors in the sun near the peach tree. Late Sunday night, I had remembered the little red shoes and brought them inside. Lured to our yard with the promise of plentiful nectar oozing from drop peaches, evidently one of the swarming bees had found shelter for the night inside our short one's shoes.

After counting a total of five stings, I removed the stinger with tweezers and thanked the Lord that our stoic little rope jumper had suffered no ill effects, only pain. A few days later, words written by Russian novelist Boris Pasternak caught my attention: "Pain makes men think, and thinking gives man wisdom; and wisdom confers peace."

Wow. For something like thirty years, I would have declared peace came both from God and from a rack (which I did not have) stuck in the dryer to keep freshly washed sneakers from thumping.

Lord, keep me alert to the pain of those around me. Help those who live under my roof gain wisdom from whatever pain need not have been. And grant me the right words at the right time to share the peace of Jesus with those who are hurting.

Chapter 20

Zap-along Cassidy

He calls his own sheep by name and leads them...and his sheep follow him because they know his voice.

—John 10:3–4, NIV

Mothers of five or more children might be better suited to the task of childrearing had we come equipped with octopus arms and eyes like birds of prey. As it is, even the best of the breed tend to have eyes more like the dragonfly, catching in multiples the closest culprit while the rest get away with, if not murder, then considerably more than they should. It might also be nice if those eyes nearly all mothers believe to be God-installed in the backs of our heads could offer less threat and more promise.

While the heads of most mothers swing easily from side to side, kids are born knowing a kazillion maneuvers for avoiding eye contact. Fail to establish eye contact, and a mom soon learns that whatever directive she meant to convey, if not dead, is badly outnumbered. While our kids quickly became pros at gazing into any eye on the horizon other than mine, this mom came with left fingers designed to snap at the drop of an out-of-sync snicker.

Being relatively quiet, finger snapping works well in church, though perhaps not in churches of the mega or deeply solemn variety. With our much moving about, most churches we've belonged to have been small and family oriented, and made up of folks who got together for potlucks or prayer meeting with equal enthusiasm.

Further, the kids who've been ours to love and to discipline were born close to the crest of the dark ages through which few church boards could agree as to whether or not nursery confinement could inflict spiritual injury on unsuspecting rug rats. Children's church had barely come into existence and was therefore suspect. Sitting quietly beside parents in church being the ultimate among assorted boredoms, kids old enough to beg successfully, and in public, generally opted for permission to sit with anyone other than a parent whose frown could hush a whispering lip into instant silence.

Today is a great day for young mothers in Churchville. While future Sunday school teachers and board members learn to take turns and bond in safe and sanitary nurseries, their unhampered moms are free to fellowship. Few have a clue on the subject of social gatherings as applied to their moms and grand-moms. Then, a big night out meant holding one kid on your lap while snapping your fingers to gain the attention of the two who were running around.

The finger-snapping system was not unlike an impromptu game of gotcha. This mom had it down pat. One snap, ears pricked, eyes swiveled, whispers ceased, kids behaved. Kids at the long distance end of a snap were not always small.

Once as we searched during prayer for a toy dropped beneath our pew, my glance happened on a scene across the aisle where Anita had been given permission to sit with a friend. While the friend's mother was absent, and her father holding forth in prayer, a sixth and a seventh grader should have done all right on her own.

As it was, the two had dropped to their knees before the pew, though not to pray. The offspring for whom I'd just purchased training bras no longer wore a small scarf knotted at her throat in the then-popular style, but had turned and drawn that wispy bit of nylon bandit-style up over her face. As I watched, one dimpled fist turned into a gun aimed at her snickering friend whose scarf had become an Indian headband, complete with pew-pencil feather. Pocahontas drew back a make-believe bow.

One snap of practiced fingers and both cowboy and Indian bit whatever dust our long-suffering custodian had failed to wipe from beneath that pew. By the time prayer had ended, gun and bow had vanished, scarves were in place, and the two sat as piously upright in their pews as had the silent Quaker ancestors of our guilty-faced young cowgirl.

After our girls grew older and had learned to obey the gentle command, the need for snapping fingers diminished. Three were singing in choir; in fact, the Sunday their two-year-old sibling broke loose and backed down a side aisle, her brown eyes begging for a game of not-so-trivial pursuit.

Patting the seat beside me, I shook my head.

She eyeballed the ceiling.

I snapped my fingers, sensed movement near the front, and glanced at the choir loft just in time to catch two altos and a longhaired soprano in the act of jerking to attention.

Like the soft snapping of a mother's fingers, God's still small voice sometimes seeks to gain my attention, to admonish or to instruct me. I wonder. Will my response be one of eager recognition? Or, like a headstrong child, am I more likely to avoid eye contact and go right on doing my own thing?

Father, like all moms, I'm busy. While I never once fitted a yellow pencil arrow into a make-believe bow beneath a pew, I find it all too easy to miss hearing your voice while tackling some task. Lord, please help me to direct my antenna to pick up your signal and then help me to listen.

Chapter 21

Chicken Noodle Scoop

A heart at peace gives life to the body, but envy rots the bones.

—Proverbs 14:30, NIV

Given a choice, I'd as soon sit a second time through all seven root canals as to go back to caring daily for other people's children. I did that for two years, and two was enough. While kids in all shapes and sizes will forever be among earth's greatest blessings, dividing my time between multiple runny noses and potty stops seemed always to subtract hours needed for my own children. Childcare dollars, however, meant I could stay at home, care for my own preschoolers (however haphazardly), and be ready with snacks and a listening ear when the older children arrived home from school.

While I tried never to let the kids catch me, I confess that those were days in which I glanced repeatedly out the window facing the direction from whence came parents. Our soon-to-be-six-year-old, on the other hand, considered each day a party. When the time came for Andie to go to school, in fact, she decided she would rather not. Denied that option, she seemed for a time to have settled into her classroom with both joy and enthusiasm.

Then one morning around 11:30, as rising bread dough plopped from bowl to counter and a couple of diapers had started to reek, the school secretary called. First graders were heading for lunch and Andrea had a little tummy ache. Could I please come and get her.

Having one crib cherub and three rug rats to look after, and with four of their kindergarten siblings due to arrive and scramble around my table for lunch at any moment, hiking off to school after an ailing child bearing my last name was no small task. Not when the only vehicle we owned happened to be at work with Norm. Difficult or not, I begged assistance from a longsuffering neighbor, ran a comb through my hair, and sprinted the quarter mile to school.

Once home, the sick one plopped herself alongside the table and slurped seconds on chicken noodle soup as noisily as did my daytime brood. Next morning, we sent her back to school.

About 11:30, as I was sucking up dirt from an overturned flower pot while two afraid-of vacuum-cleaners rug rats screamed, and a third helped herself to a chew off my prayer plant, guess what? The phone rang. Again, I called my neighbor, ran a comb through my hair, and et cetera. Again, the one with the pain in her midsection devoured a hearty lunch.

Following a third summons to school, I got smart (or so I thought), tucked a small dose of kid-pink antacid called Pepto Bismol into her Cinderella lunch box, and did a little telephoning of my own.

"Have her take it around eleven," I said to the school nurse. "That should soothe her stomach in time for lunch."

For three consecutive days, the plan worked.

On the fourth day, when the ringing began at 11:30, without touching the phone, I knew who was calling.

"Your little one is vomiting blood," a distraught secretary warbled. "The nurse isn't in and I don't know what to do."

Needless to say, I yelled for my neighbor to come at once, dispensed with hair combing, and literally flew to the school.

Our fourth-born lay on a cot in a room adjoining the office. All things and her pale face considered, any moment could mean sad farewell.

"Are you sure about the blood?" I asked the secretary in a frightened whisper.

"See for yourself," she said, leading me to a basin in the office lavatory.

One glance and relief hit like the proverbial ton of bricks. At the same time, I bounced from beneath those bricks biting my tongue and seething over having been so disrupted. How could a grown person, one who dealt daily with children, possibly mistake the pink froth of regurgitated Pepto Bismol for blood?

At the secretary's insistence, I took my daughter home and made an appointment with our doctor.

After hearing my story and examining the ailing one, the doctor invited me into his office for the best advice I have ever followed for dealing with kids looking for an excuse to skip school.

Armed for life with his best advice, the next time the secretary called, I walked the blonde one home and told her to go get dressed in her pajamas and climb immediately into bed. I explained that I could no longer risk having her expose other children to whatever it was that ailed her. Then I kissed her, tucked a warm comforter beneath her startled chin, walked out, and closed the door behind me. Miraculously healed, she was not only well enough to attend school the next day, but to stay there.

Much later, after she had matured enough to be totally truthful, I asked this kid, who now seemed to prefer school to home, what had caused her to repeatedly fake being sick.

"I wasn't faking," she insisted. "The minute I smelled our school lunch cooking, I would think about the chicken noodle soup you would be fixing for all those other kids, and then I couldn't eat my sandwich."

"But we didn't have chicken noodle soup every day. Possibly every two weeks; maybe even less."

"I know, Mom. But if there was even a remote chance those other kids got to enjoy my favorite, the chicken noodle soup lover inside me simply couldn't handle cheese or peanut butter or whatever else you'd sent with me for lunch."

As has been said, "The ear of jealousy heareth all things" (*Apocrypha* The Wisdom of Solomon, chapter

1, verse 5). But the sound of a can opener riding the rim of a soup can? Preposterous.

Lord, a little nourishment and even a touch of envy can turn into a green-eyed monster of dissention and destruction. Thank you for a family in which envy never grew any bigger than a can of Campbell's soup.

Heard through an open bedroom door in the midst of a my-side your-side territorial scrap. "I hope if God ever lets you into heaven, he gives you a room all by yourself 700 miles down the hall!"

Chapter 22

Sit Not

A greedy man brings trouble to his family.
—Proverbs 15:27, NIV

"A television would be nice to have," I thought the day I laid aside good sense long enough to assure still another young working mother that, for five days each week, I would try adding one babe-in-arms and two little boys to a household already replete with a new baby and multiple children of our own. Programs such as *Sesame Street,* I reasoned, could buy me a little time for something besides changing diapers and settling kid scraps. My decision to again take on childcare, however, was not for the purpose of buying a TV or anything else, but to help my partner in life keep ahead of the bills.

They were sweet children, and good. They were also needy, especially Bernie, the oldest, who had a speech problem. "I don't want to leave them," their mother had confided the day she came to check out this babysitter and our home. Perched on the edge of her chair, her thin hands shredding an already tattered pink tissue, she reminded me of a frightened little bird about to take flight.

Watching her dab at her eyes, (knowing this was hardly a way to gain business), I asked, "Have you thought about doing childcare in your home? You can earn just as much and, at the same time, be home with your own children."

"Oh, no, I couldn't," she replied—so hastily I could tell she had either tried or had wanted to try that route. "Royce can hardly put up with our own children."

Remembering how precious our girls were to my spouse, I felt sorry for having to explain, "I'm not sure I can handle another baby along with my own and still keep an eye on five other children, but we'll give it a try for three weeks. If we see it's not working, I'll say so, and you can find someone else."

"Royce will drop me off at the laundry just before eight—that's the only place I could find work—and then he'll bring them," she said. "We just have the pickup."

As she stood to go, I noticed her unlined jacket and worn summer sandals. Cold continued to fill the house long after I had closed the door behind her. In the kitchen, I peered at the indoor-outdoor thermometer, then glanced at the clock. At 11 A.M. on this January day, the mercury still hung below zero.

Monday morning, Royce brought the children as expected. It had snowed all day Sunday and well into the night. With all that must be done before leaving for work, Norm had not found time to shovel the front sidewalk. Failing to notice the wide shoveled path to the back door, the door we almost always used, Royce stopped beside the front entrance, lifted the boys from pickup to snowdrift and pointed to the front door before picking up the baby.

The weather still being extremely cold, I hurried the boys inside, leaving the door ajar long enough for Royce to hand me the baby. Dumping a diaper bag at my feet, he turned abruptly. "Ain't fit for a man to be out," he muttered as he left the porch and plowed back through the snow to the pickup.

After unwinding a worn blanket from the baby, I laid her in the playpen and turned to the boys still shivering beside the front door. Small wonder! Clad in blue gabardine jackets as thin as their mother's, neither wore cap or mittens and neither had on socks. Lifting first Billy, then Bernie onto the couch, I removed their wet sneakers and cupped their icy feet for a moment in my hands before pulling a warm afghan around them.

"Sit here and get warm," I said and hurried upstairs to bring socks from our own children's meager supply.

An hour later the sneakers had dried and were back on the boys' feet. While I was busier than ever, "busy" was what I had anticipated. But when Royce came after the children a little before five, and I noticed his sheepskin lined coat and warm cap, a day that had gone well started to turn sour.

Tuesday evening, as I helped the children into their wraps, Anita ran to her room. When Royce started to leave with the children, she thrust a pair of red mittens at Bernie and said, "Here, wear these."

"Nah. He don't need mittens. He's a little man," Royce said.

"It's OK. I have two pair. He can have these," she insisted. Edging away from Royce, she touched Bernie with the mittens.

"No, he can't," Royce snarled. Grabbing the baby, pushing the boys ahead with a neatly polished boot, he stepped out, slamming the door behind him.

A week or so later, as Royce lingered to talk, I asked, "What kind of work do you do?"

"Me? I don't. I got this disability, see…"

I couldn't see, but then there are many kinds of disabilities, and certain ones cannot be seen.

"I bet yur wonderin' if yur gonna get paid. Yur go'n' to all right, but not till the wife gets hers. My disability check takes care o' me just fine, but I got no extra."

He grinned. "Matter o' fact, that's why I got 'er workin'. The days get long when a man cain't work and I'm needin' me a new TV."

I suppose it was none of my business but, "Royce," I protested, "the children need warm coats and socks."

Pulling on sleek leather gloves, he picked up the baby. "They'd just grow out of 'em," he whined. The middle of week three, he actually had the audacity to report, "The missus got paid Friday but she ain't makin' much. Hit took nearly her whole check to pay for the TV. We'll catch you next time."

They didn't; never did, in fact. At the end of my promised three weeks, enough was enough. Somehow, knowing Royce's wife and children would remain needy no matter what I did, I couldn't see working to buy any more stuff for a grown man.

The truth is, after those three weeks of babysitting, while I'd gathered up some used clothing for the boys and helped to buy a new television (albeit unwillingly), our children would not be watching *Sesame Street*, not for a couple of years anyhow. What's more, Norm and I were in full agreement. We never did find it necessary for me to leave the kids and go get a job just to buy a TV or any other doodad.

Lord, my prayer today is for young parents everywhere. Help each couple to weigh carefully those reasons behind a decision to become a two-income family. I pray for warm mittens and for socks enough to clothe a world of children. And please, Lord, help me never again to find myself in the role of enabler. One more thing, Lord—please look out for little ones everywhere who must snuggle up to a TV to warm cold fingers.

Chapter 23

Spaghetti Oh-Oh

May the words of my mouth and the meditation of my heart be pleasing in your sight, O Lord, my Rock and my Redeemer.

—Psalm 19:14, NIV

They had never been our favorite dinner guests. Their three boys fought like rattlesnakes with their tails tied together and could dream up orneriness faster than a street gang. We attended the same small church, however, and the parents were our friends.

I kept the menu simple: Chunky homemade meat sauce over spaghetti, tossed green salad, and garlic bread, with a family favorite called "crazy cake" for dessert.

Had I stirred pasta and sauce together loblolly style the way our family likes it, the dinner might have gone all right. Instead, I chose to go with spaghetti according to my own preference, spaghetti fixed in a way our older kids sneeringly referred to as "blah."

Sauce bubbled near the brim of an oversized electric skillet and I had cooked enough American Beauty spaghetti to feed a small church camp by the time our guests arrived.

The day being uncommonly warm for late September, the children begged to eat outdoors. After calling them in to wash their hands and then to fill their plates, I rummaged in the refrigerator for our hodgepodge of salad dressings.

"Billy doesn't like pasta. May I help myself to a bowl so he can have some sauce?" my friend Donna asked. The request was not uncommon; kids often say "Yuck" to any cooking other than their mom's—especially Maxwell and Donna's kids.

"Sure, help yourself," I said, doling out French bread, noting that the children's plates were typical—a whole lot of pasta colored by a little bit of sauce and flanked by traces of salad bowl favorites laced generously with dressing.

Then came Billy.

While Donna cautioned, "Be careful, son, don't spill," I stared in disbelief. The bowl Donna's second born carried had been filled to the brim. Donna had not given him a sauce dish or soup bowl, but a serving bowl big enough to hold spaghetti sauce for a family three times our size. The bowl must have contained at least a pound of meat along with all the other ingredients that go into the making of a fine spaghetti sauce.

"This stuff smells good. I'll come back and get my bread," Billy announced with an innocent grin while his mother held the screen door open for him.

As it turned out, eleven-year-old Billy didn't care for salad either, or chocolate cake. Billy's meal consisted of half of the spaghetti sauce intended to serve twelve and the soft centers pulled from eight slices of French bread.

With effort, I zipped my mouth and removed a pile of warm plates from the oven for the adults. Spreading to make the skimpier-than-planned servings look better, I spooned what was left of the sauce over generous heaps of steaming pasta.

Halfway through the meal, Maxwell held out his plate. "That's mighty fine sauce. Could I have a trace more to help finish off this wad of pasta?" he asked.

Embarrassed to have to explain I was sorry but the sauce was all gone, I should have explained and allowed the matter to drop. However, I was mad. Mad at Billy for being such a pig. Mad at Donna for allowing him to be one. And mad at myself for not having taken control of my own household the minute I'd seen Billy head outdoors with that big dish of sauce.

To compensate for what our main meal lacked, I dipped ice cream intended for Tuesday's night's out-of-town guests alongside the cake, faked a two-hour smile that barely lasted until our dinner guests were out the door, and vowed never again to invite them for a meal.

"Look, Mom, Billy wasted a whole bunch of perfectly good spaghetti sauce," a daughter complained as we cleaned up the kitchen. That's when I discovered the eight crusty wheels of bread with which Billy had decorated the half-bowl of sauce he'd probably gotten too full to eat.

"Never mind," I muttered, thinking all the while that it was I who minded and who minded a whole lot.

"Grief. You'd never let us do stuff like that."

"You're not company," I retorted, and couldn't resist adding, "you're our own good little girl, and you've already learned it's not nice to be selfish and wasteful." One way or another I would get said what I was thinking.

Another daughter entered the kitchen.

"Look," said the first, "selfish pig Billy hogged the spaghetti sauce and then wasted it."

"Shush. No name calling," I said.

She looked at me wide-eyed. "Mo-o-om, you said so yourself."

While her interpretation differed considerably from what I had actually said, she had a point. Further, the thought occurred to me that a bad attitude might easily cause more damage than all the bad manners in the world.

Next morning, Donna brought over a bushel of late tomatoes from her garden and said maybe they'd make good spaghetti sauce. And the next time we invited her family to come for dinner, I made it a point to ask what her boys liked best to eat.

Fine-lining a menu in advance left a much better taste in my mouth than had attempts to cover a bad attitude with artificial sweet talk or having to swallow unkind words.

Lord, a household the size of ours gets smacked pretty often with a generous supply of petty irritations. Add more kids, and the potential for aggravation gets worse. What I need, Lord, is not fewer children or irritations, but a mind quick enough to always remember to set a good example and to change my actions or slap a hand over my mouth whenever I don't.

Crazy Cake

3 c. sifted flour
1 tsp. salt
2 tsp. baking soda
2 c. sugar
6 tbsp. cocoa
¾ c. cooking oil
2 tbsp. vinegar
2 tsp. vanilla

Spray 9" × 13" pan with cooking spray. Sift dry ingredients together. Add wet ingredients. Pour 2 cups cold water over all. Beat until well mixed. Pour batter into pan and bake about 40 minutes, 350 degrees. Cool and frost with One-Minute Fudge Frosting.

One-minute Fudge Frosting

1 c. sugar
¼ c. cocoa
¼ c. margarine
¼ c. milk

Mix. Bring to rolling boil. Boil 1 minute exactly. Cool, beating some until frosting reaches spreading consistency. Spread rapidly on cake.
Note: If frosting sugars or hardens too rapidly, add 1 tbsp. milk and reheat. When doubling the recipe, boil for 2 minutes.

Chapter 24

Head Gear

A man's ways are in full view of the Lord.

—Proverbs 5:21, NIV

At thirteen—that terrible year of suspension between child and adulthood—the tall one was old enough to baby sit, too young to drive, and often a pain to live with. Possessed with moods (temporary, we hoped) that changed more often than she donned clean socks, she could blow us away with attitudes that fluctuated from glum to glorious to gruesome in no seconds flat.

In the room she shared with her sisters, a tangle of empty hangers along with a wide-open door marked the spot where her clothes had once hung neatly from a bar at her end of the closet. We're not talking outgrown dungarees or soiled blouses, or even speaking of the grimy wadded sock beneath the edge of her unmade bed. We're talking big time careless—clothes trampled underfoot, traded with friends, lost, given away, or rendered less than wearable in ways too untidy to mention.

In the midst of the chaos characterizing both her inner and outer life came spring volleyball season and the girls' opening game scheduled at a school other than our own. As was customary, the visiting team (our daughter's) dressed down using the boys' locker room. The game went well, her team won, and nothing other than the ordinary happened until Sunday morning.

"Mom, have you seen my pettipants?" the once-orderly one called from her bedroom.

I had not.

"Weren't they in the wash?"

"No," I replied without hesitation.

"Are you sure?"

The load of delicates in Friday's laundry had consisted of the usual smaller unmentionables. No pettipants, not even a slip or dainty sweater.

"I'm sure."

"Well, they have to be someplace!"

Given her latest attitude concerning the care and pressing of clothing, the garment could be anyplace. Still, knowing the lace-trimmed, latest fashion bit of lingerie had been a Christmas gift and was special to her, I choked down a tongue full of snide comments on the subject of wardrobe care and helped her look. But getting a family out the door in time to teach a sixth-grade Sunday school class left little time for dealing with crises.

Besides, I had problems of my own. I worried through church, in fact, because April 15 was fast approaching and I had yet to lay hands on a W-2 form I distinctly recalled having carried from mailbox to house with my very own hand. For a careless teenager to suffer through worship minus an undergarment unlikely to be seen beyond bath or bedroom seemed minor in comparison to standing formless before a looming tax deadline.

Someone has said that there is seldom a loss without some small gain. That week, the ironing board came out and the floor began to show once more in the girls' bedroom. But volleyball season was still in full swing, and the tournament barely three weeks away.

"All I have time for is practice and homework," the deprived one wailed. "I can't even babysit and earn money for new pettipants."

"How about using what little bit of time you do have to help me look for the W-2 form," I suggested. "Maybe we'll find your pettipants while we're looking."

"Fun-ny."

She had a right to sarcasm. The truth was, while my situation had all but reached the point of desperation, hers was heartbreaking. Neither of us felt much like laughing.

Tournament time came and went and that evening the tall one barely made it home in time to wash her hands before dinner. As we sat down, I laughed and rejoiced and confessed to having located the lost W-2 form in a box of stuff on the back porch—a box into which, two months earlier, I had shoved stuff off counters and tabletops in a desperate rush to prepare for guests I had known were coming for at least a week.

"So, how was the tournament?" the father of our brood asked as soon as he could get in a word.

"OK. We got second place," the tall one replied in a tone that said something had gone terribly wrong.

"What's the matter?" I asked.

"Mom—just leave me alone and let me die," she wailed.

Having been through numerous death scenes with the sibling who'd turned thirteen two years before the wailing one, I suggested she at least offer an explanation suitable for inclusion in her obituary.

In the end, it was the sister one grade below her who told.

"These boys from Mountain View School ran out onto the field between games," she said. "They were waving stuff in the air, hollering and carrying on—you know how dumb boys can be—and daring girls from other schools to come claim their stuff. The last guy in line had a pair of white pettipants—" She popped a hand over her mouth to stifle a giggle.

"It's not funny!"

"Yes, it is," the short one said as soon as she could stop giggling long enough to speak. "He was wearing them on his head."

"You claimed them, of course?" a dad struggling for control said to the mortified one after the laughter had died down.

"Daddy! That would have been too embarrassing."

Now that volleyball season with its long hours of practice had come to an end, she could go back to babysitting and, unless pettipants went out of fashion right away, she would soon have money saved for a new pair. If not, she had at least started to take better care of her clothes.

That same week I drove down to Wal-Mart and bought a red accordion file large enough to hold a lot of stuff. I sorted all that was worth keeping out of the box from the back porch and threw the box away. We haven't lost track of a W-2 form since.

Lord, being a God of order and not of confusion, even though you knew where the stuff was, you let us seek for a while before allowing us to find. And, while the tall one seems to have learned her lesson, you know far better than I that one lost and found W-2 form is not likely to transform my willy-nilly ways, not even if I should catch sight of our CPA wearing said form on his head. So keep working on me, Lord. And help me never to, not in all my careless doings, cause you shame.

Twice the preceding week, I had stitched the torn-loose sash back in place and now I was sewing it again, this time with a double seam.

Later, while talking with a friend on the phone, I mentioned the torn sash and wondered aloud what sort of play was being allowed on the school playground.

"Oh, don't blame the school," my friend said. "If what my son told me is true, it may be his fault. I think he's figured out what sashes are good for."

The children were current best friends. Our daughter, in fact, had a crush on my friend's little boy. "Oh?"

She laughed. "He tells me over and over again that Jennifer is the best horse in the second grade. Each time you have to sew a sash back on it may be because my son has gotten a bit heavy handed with his gee's and his haw's."

Chapter 25

Sweet Harmony

Therefore, as God's chosen people, holy and dearly loved, clothe yourselves with compassion, kindness, humility, gentleness and patience.

—Colossians 3:12, NIV

Three work-free days interspersed with nightmares pretty much describes the house hunting trips offered by my beloved's mega company employer after said company's powers-that-be had already decided what was to become of us. We who got moved so often seldom had to change furnace filters, and adding a church search to a fast-forward gander through houses and schools meant having to trust God for instant guidance. This time, our patient head-of-household had had to handle the entire go-around on his own.

"The church is small but enthusiastic," he said after telling me about our next house, a two-story located in the same town and almost identical to Ronald Regan's birthplace.

No problem. We'd belonged to churches having limited resources before and were used to serving.

He cleared his throat. "Uh—the church folks are wonderful—uh, really loving."

I had heard him clear his throat in like manner on other occasions: the day the radiator fell out of the car while he was playing "dune buggy" among some old strip mines. The evening he accidentally spray-painted the baby. I waited.

"They—uh—don't have a pianist. I told them—honey, I told them you'd play."

Sounding, I'm sure, like the mother of all shrews, I screeched, "You what? You know I can't play that well!"

"Sweetheart, you're a maestro compared to what they have. Believe me. One lady is taking piano lessons. She picks out notes with one finger. The pastor's wife tries, but she herself refers to her own best attempt as 'awful.'"

Great. So now the sprouting little congregation was to be blessed with a trio of incompetents.

In fairness, having grown up in a non-musical family, my well-meaning spouse with his gift of helps had no clue that his fascination with my jazzy version of *Sentimental Journey* in no way qualified me to serve as church musician.

Further, all twelve of my piano lessons happened during grammar school and were mine through transaction. Our neighbor owned a whole lot of cows and taught piano. Dad had a whole lot of kids and owned pasture. Their ensuing agreement meant that, for two summers, my sisters and I enjoyed bi-weekly piano lessons at the elbow of gray-haired, maiden lady Florence. Along with cows, Florence must also have been blessed with unlimited patience. How else could she have taught piano to three barefooted kids who had only a wheezy old treadle organ on which to practice?

The day my beloved sprang his musical surprise, we owned neither piano nor organ. Further, since the onset of motherhood, I had seldom, if ever, sat down before a keyboard.

We arrived at our new location on a Saturday. Surrounded by boxes, yet desiring to worship, I showered and dressed early the next morning before waking the family. Failing to locate slippers, I donned an old pair of flats left over from college days. Speckled with paint from two kitchens back, they were more practical than pumps as I searched for our church clothes.

Following a canned applesauce and toast-minus-butter breakfast, and an unheard of skipping of Sunday school, we finally got ourselves passably dressed for our less-than-grand entrance into a tiny sanctuary furnished mostly with piano, pulpit, and assorted folding chairs. All nineteen necks craned as we shooed kids onto a donated pew near the back of the small building that was to become our church home for two years.

"Wait," the pastor said as a sweet-faced woman arose and moved to the piano. "I believe our new pianist has arrived. Welcome, sister. You have no idea how fervently we have prayed for someone to relieve my wife and this congregation from her misery."

While everyone laughed, including the wife, his kind glance traveled from me to the congregation. "Let's join in the *Doxology* while the good sister comes to the piano," he said, and proceeded to lead.

What could I do other than go with the flow? While they sang "Praise God from whom all blessings," dark thoughts rippled near flood stage as I begged God on my way to a makeshift platform for "Please, no more than three sharps."

Later, I would suggest we should have begun with *Amazing Grace* because, to my astonishment, I breezed through every song and a passable offertory without making a single serious mistake. By the time we'd sung the last song and I'd breathed my own prayer of thanks during the benediction, I had started to feel better. If I really was the best pianist available, perhaps with God's help and a little practice, I could fill in for a time.

That decided, I stepped from the platform and discovered in a fraction of an instant what it means to die a thousand deaths. In my haste to get our family put together for the day, I had forgotten to change shoes!

While our new church family gathered to welcome us, I petitioned God under my breath to please not let anyone notice those paint-spattered shoes.

It was silly to pray such a prayer in the aisle of a beginning church that boasted no modesty skirt beside its piano (a church, I might add, that I soon learned felt blessed even to own a piano). For something like half of the worship hour, my shoes had been in plain view of the entire congregation. Anyone glancing in my direction had surely already seen them and seen the paint.

Equally foolish was my assumption that worn-out shoes or paint spatters could make any difference. My marriage partner had been right. This loving, welcoming congregation laughed with me and not at me. What's more, those folks never did get themselves a "real" piano player, at least not until after we'd been transferred to another location.

Thinking back, those good people had to have been like those mentioned in Colossians, clothed with compassion, kindness, and gentleness. It almost goes without saying that they also practiced patience three or more times a week while I grew in humility as I listened to their attempts to keep in sync with this amateur musician.

Thank you, Lord, for grace!

Having spent half a morning engrossed in a catalog, Andrea showed me pictures of the four dolls she wanted for Christmas "so I can play family like ours," she told me.

"I thought you were mad at your sisters," I teased.

"I am," she said, "but they still make a really good family."

Chapter 26

Cause and Effect

The Lord gives wisdom, and from his mouth come knowledge and understanding...Discretion will protect you, and understanding will guard you. Wisdom will save you from the ways of wicked men.

—Proverbs 2:6; 11–12b, NIV

Most families include at least one child with a need to insert one thing or another into his or her mouth for the purpose of sucking his or her way toward comfort or contentment. Our family began with a thumb sucker. Then came one who departed the womb with two fingers tucked into her mouth and another two jabbing at her big blue eyes. A third got her kicks from humming and sucking blisters onto a forefinger while flicking her nose with the saliva-stiffened corner of a satin-bound blanket.

Scorning thumbs, fingers, and blankets, the obstinate one opted instead to grind ice begged from family water glasses between her first teeth. Sandwiched among all these came the child who not only nuzzled up to the zigzag seam of her blanket binding but who glommed onto anything else she could cram between her lips.

When the time came for us to make our longest distance move, because the child with a mouth full of doodads was going on three, we sold her crib. We also dispensed with a set of rickety bunk beds. Once we reached our destination, the children slept on mattresses on the floor until we found time to shop for beds. Since rolling off a mattress might prove traumatic for one accustomed to a crib, we put Chipmunk Cheeks next to the wall where we figured she could chew on her blanket binding and fight sleep to her heart's content.

One day, after sending her sisters for some quiet time in the living room with books, I tucked her in for her nap as usual. The children's bedroom being separated from the kitchen by only a short hall, I could hear the rhythmic thumping of a foot kicking the wall as I stood at the sink cleaning vegetables for stew. When the thumping ceased, I assumed our blonde one had again lost her twice-daily battle with Mr. Sandman.

Moments later, as I reached for the cold water faucet, I heard the unmistakable sounds of sizzling and crackling followed by a short but distinct pop. Dropping the paring knife, I bolted through acrid-smelling air to the children's room.

Hand outstretched, our little one stared mutely up at me from her place on the mattress. Behind her, just inches from where she should have been sleeping, a slender spiral of smoke curled from a blackened electrical outlet.

Snatching her up in my arms, I gently pried open the tiny hand. She whimpered. Recognizing the misshapen remains of a pink plastic barrette that had melted and stuck to her wee pink palm, I moaned. A still-wet barrette and the marks seared by what was left of a wire clasp told the story: Searching as always for something to chew on, she had worked the barrette loose, stuck it in her mouth, and then discovered that the outlet holes were just right for poking.

Aware of how fortunate we were to be hearing her cry, I carried her to the kitchen and lowered my trembling self onto a kitchen chair while the rest of the children gathered to pat their sister and gape at her injury. Being the mom, I closed my eyes, took a few deep breaths and, except for knees that shook for the rest of the day, pulled myself together. Gingerly lifting one end of the barrette, I noted with relief that the melted plastic was attached only in one small spot. Before I could lose my nerve, as gently and quickly as possible, I pulled the plastic loose and sprayed the raw spot with anesthetic burn ointment to ease the pain.

Hearing a swishing sound near my elbow, I turned in time to witness a thud. Unable to bear the sight of her sister's discomfort, the one with the blistered forefinger had passed out at my feet.

The faint one survived, of course, as did the injured one. We invested in outlet covers and I doubled what I'd wrongly assumed to be adequate safety measures. Years passed before any one among our brood found courage to plug in even legitimate objects without supervision.

As time passed, the brown marks seared across the blonde one's fingers served to remind all of us that poking even so much as the tip of a barrette into whatever God has marked "unsafe" comes with natural consequences.

And, for a while, a bump on the back of our short one's head gave credence to the fact that what we do does matter and really can affect the other person.

Lord, thank you for the abiding presence of the Holy Spirit, who keeps us from harm and guides us so that we need never submit to temptation. Clothe us daily in armor suited to a child of God, then surround us with guardian angels and protect us from the compelling power of our own curiosity.

Chapter 27

Berry Funny

You may be sure that your sin will find you out.

—Numbers 32:23b, NIV

Gooseberries (those sour little pellets with the striped green skin) are low on my list when it comes to edible fruit. However, I have only to *think* gooseberries to bring on the tart-sweet taste of the heavenly pale pink concoction my mother called gooseberry jell. So when my sis offered gooseberries from her garden, my memory did a jelly jog and I gladly accepted the two or so quarts she sent home with me in a plastic ice cream bucket.

At home, having been reared on a farm by not one, but two green-thumbed parents, I took one look at those gooseberries and remembered that most fruits remain at their luscious best only if canned, frozen, jellied, or jammed in their prime. What I knew, however, I could not always do. Not with five kids to tend and a spouse who sometimes traveled on his job as a corrosion specialist almost as widely as I spread peanut butter. Still, the gooseberries had started to ripen.

"You'll have to help," I said next day to my mobile four over the tousled head of a cranky baby after the washer had growled once and resigned.

The day being hot, we dragged lawn chairs to where the back porch joined the house and I showed them how to pinch off gooseberry stems and rub away dried blossoms with their thumbs. I then phoned Sears & Roebuck's service department, rinsed and wrung wet baby clothes by hand. Since we had no clothes dryer at the time, as I pinned them to the line, I thanked God for Norm and the clothesline he kept in good repair.

I had barely started to rock the teething one before I heard the slap of thongs and the cheerful voice of our thirteen-year-old calling to me from the kitchen.

"We're done, Mom."

"Already?"

"Stemming gooseberries is cinchy."

Book in hand, she flopped onto her bed to read while the rest returned to their play. Thinking I might have time to make jelly before I needed to start dinner, I gave the now-quiet baby a teething biscuit and plopped her into her playpen.

On the kitchen counter beside the empty ice cream bucket sat the large bowl into which my inexperienced berry crew were supposed to have dropped the stemmed berries. Noting that the bottom of the bowl was barely covered, I called the girls, waited until all four had gathered into a guilty-faced line, then asked, "What happened to the rest of the gooseberries?"

One giggled nervously, another scratched the back of her leg, and the other two eyed each other.

"That's all there were," one said.

"Eight cups is equal to two quarts. We had two quarts. They came to here," I said, marking the bucket with a forefinger.

"They had lotsa stems."

"Some were no good."

"What did you do with the no good ones?" I asked.

"Dumped them in the burning barrel," the middle one confessed, referring to a barrel near the back fence where we sometimes burned trash.

The barrel being past due for a dumping, the fruit was near the top and easy to spot. Ashes could be washed off.

By the time the gritty-faced culprits had retrieved, washed, stemmed, and rubbed blossoms from more than five additional cups of jell-perfect gooseberries, the berries had to be refrigerated and my jelly-making postponed until morning.

In spite of the discard history of those gooseberries, the jelly turned out to be the ambrosia among assorted jellies and jams that got made and stored on a shelf in the basement that summer.

Come spring, as I raked away winter's debris from the corner between the porch and the house, I discovered that not all of those gooseberries had landed in the barrel; some had fallen on good ground. Among the grape hyacinth and lily-of-the-valley were hundreds of tiny new plants with dainty scalloped leaves. For as long as we lived in that house, we pulled gooseberry sprouts.

What's more, for quite some time, no child had to remind another that wrongdoing has a way of tattling on itself. All one had to say was "gooseberries," and the four who had spent quality time with those gooseberries got the point.

Lord, sometimes the blunders made by our children are so funny there is no way we can keep from laughing with them. Thank you for laughter and for reminding us, even in the midst of our hilarity that, where wrongdoing is involved, we must hold those you have entrusted to us accountable. For it is through learning to be accountable to parents that children will one day find it easier to be accountable to you. And, Lord, please, may all their childish lies have to do with objects as easily disposed of as inanimate gooseberries, and not with vulnerable people.

Like most growing girls, Jennifer had hit that stage of adolescence where her daddy was her best beau, her hero, and the person of the opposite sex with whom she could safely flirt.

Once as she breezed by, patted his cheek, and kissed him on top of the head, her little sister Renee looked up from her play, gave her a sober look, and said, "I wouldn't kiss him if I were you. He's married."

Chapter 28

Babe 'n' Butterfly

Therefore, if anyone is in Christ, he is a new creation; the old has gone, the new has come!

—2 Corinthians 5:17, NIV

"Goodnight!" "Get back in your bed." "Don't let me see your face again."

Four bedtime stories, three drinks of water, repeated hugs, and a steady barrage of gentle threats and promises, and still the small one could not get to sleep.

We looked at each other, sighed, and prayed our silent prayers. Due to a physical disorder, nocturnal wanderings for this child were not the same as the inevitable and often manipulative pop-outs all parents of preschool children discover they must learn to count on as well as deal with.

The late news ended with a plea to join tomorrow's walkathon, and still we could hear the sound of skinny bare feet thumping rhythmically against a carved maple headboard.

While my road-weary spouse turned off the television and locked the back door, I debated. Nights when she was like this almost always meant sliding from between sheets before my bedside light had had time to cool. Should I stay up and read for a while?

"Would you come look at this?" Norm called from the family room where he'd gone to close a window.

In the family room, still damp from its cocoon, a butterfly of magnificent proportions teetered atop a pleated lampshade.

"So much for housekeeping," I started to say as Norm pointed silently to the broken shell clinging to the backside of the lampshade. But the sight of that brand new creature was too awesome.

Thoughts of sleep departed as we watched the butterfly inch ever so slightly ahead, then pause to flex its orange and black wings.

A whisper of clown-sprinkled seersucker announced that the butterfly and we were no longer alone. "Why are the lights going off and you're still up?" the small one demanded.

"Come over here by Daddy if you'd like to see a miracle," her father said, lifting her for a closer look.

She giggled. "That's not a mir'cle; that's a butterfly. A Monarch. My bug book gots a picture of a Monarch."

Her giggling stopped and she lapsed into wide-eyed silence as the butterfly began slowly making its way around the rim of the lampshade.

She started to reach for it, but drew back as the beautiful insect fluttered away from her grasp and lit on her dad's arm.

"Where'd it come from?" she wanted to know.

Showing her the torn casing, I explained, "The butterfly was once a worm."

"That's the miracle," her dad interjected. "Worm. Butterfly."

She listened raptly as we explained in simple terms how metamorphosis takes place. Then, while the butterfly teetered on a makeshift landing field and continued with its flight preparation, I grabbed the camera and snapped a picture.

The living room clock chimed 11:30. Six A.M. was going to come early.

Reluctantly, being careful not to touch the still-damp wings, we brushed the butterfly onto a magazine, trooped outside, and gently lifted the fragile creature onto the leaf of a pink hollyhock growing beside the carport.

As I tucked our small one back into bed, we talked some more about the miracle of butterflies. She yawned a few times, hunched into a satisfied ball, and immediately fell asleep.

Next day, she and I visited our library and brought home a brightly illustrated book about butterflies. Before the day ended, we all had a turn at reading the book to her and examining its pictures. I read it to her again at bedtime, and again she fell asleep with ease. Eventually, after the pattern had been repeated several nights in a row, we accepted the obvious: for whatever reason, the butterfly experience had been soothing.

Like the butterfly, Jesus too spent time in a darkened tomb before bursting forth in the splendor of having won a forever victory over sin. Because of his willingness to die for our sins, even the worst among us can move from sin's prison into the freedom of new life made possible through the death and resurrection of our Lord Jesus Christ.

As time passed, Renee forgot her fascination with the butterfly and the serendipitous nights of unbroken sleep came to an end. Thankfully, the miracle of salvation is not so easily dispensed with. For as "we walk in the light, as he is in the light...the blood of Jesus, his Son, purifies us from every sin" (1 John 1:7, NIV).

What a miracle!

Thank you, Lord, for butterflies and for babes in Christ everywhere who enjoy the beauty of a new life because of you.

Chapter 29

Crash Course

A friend loves at all times.

—Proverbs 17:17, NIV

Couple desperation with a trace of stupidity and even the best of multiple-kid mothers could show up at a Thursday night baby shower with a fifteen-month-old toddler in tow. The same night I had secretly planned for a two-hour escape from responsibility, the dad to our all-female brood was out of town and our born-to-the-task baby sitter came home from school swamped with homework.

"No problem," I assured the one who had so cheerfully pinch-hit for this mom on a number of occasions. I would take our little one's favorite toys and she would play quietly at my feet.

The new baby being on display as the evening began, the plan worked for about twenty minutes. The focus changed after a visiting grandmother declared an end to the brief social debut of the baby and whisked him away to an upstairs bedroom.

"Come see me," coaxed the buxom matron to my left as our gregarious toddler sat quietly cupping her favorite hollow blocks.

Ready as always for friendly interchange, she studied the matron's soft triple chins, then lifted her arms. The dear lady had no way of knowing how little it took to set this one off into perpetual, though seldom rhythmic, motion.

The minute a young woman who had no children of her own began a game of "I'magonnagetchoo," our cherub was off and running. Several times as gifts were being unwrapped, I caught and held her on my lap, attempting to quiet her.

With my attention tuned to ooh-ahing over a wee yellow sun suit, I cannot say at precisely which moment she escaped. All I remember is that I hit the carpet running the minute I heard the crash.

In the dining room, our toddler danced backwards on tiptoe beyond where splintered glass from what looked like a thousand matched snack trays littered the hardwood floor. As she stood petrified against a freshly papered wall, glass shards stabbed at her shoelaces and sparkled against wispy dark hair. Snatching her to me, I examined her face and eyes and, seeing that she was unharmed, hugged her fiercely.

The mess, however, was another matter. On the table, an empty punch bowl near teeter stage and a lace tablecloth pulled askew told the story. Too young and too short to be curious about what might be on the table, our little one had probably taken a corner too fast and grabbed onto the tablecloth to maintain balance.

Apologizing to the hostess, I plopped the reason for my red face into a high chair, dumped Cheerios from a cereal box produced by the same hostess onto its tray and swept up every visible speck of that glass. The trashing of several assorted snack trays with matching cups being no small item, I telephoned my friend in the morning and offered once more to replace them.

She laughed. "You're not going to believe this, but I don't really care for those trays. A couple of those came from store closeouts—you know how I love a bargain—and some were destined for my next yard sale, so forget it."

"Are you sure?"

"The truth is, with so many pretties available, I'd much rather use paper. But when you own snack trays, you feel obligated to use them. Thanks to your little sweetie, my conscience is clear. I can be more creative with paper."

While the trays were not a pricey item, and were often on sale, replacing five or six sets would have, for sure, punched hunger pangs in my already lean grocery budget.

"Please, don't fret another minute. Just be thankful with me that your little one was not hurt," my friend added, bringing relief to my conscience.

Grateful for her Christ-like acceptance of what we both realized had been accidental, I shoved the incident to the back of my mind and tried harder than ever to keep perpetual track of my children. Years later, a snatch of overheard conversation revealed the rest of the story.

Circumstances had changed for both of us. She now lived in an even lovelier home and I no longer had to pinch Lincoln's bronze nose before making a purchase. Still, I wanted to let her know I knew.

Again, she laughed. "I was aware of your financial struggles," she said. "You see, I had been there myself and had more than once experienced the awkwardness of owing a friend and having no money to pay. The blessing, dear friend, was mine, for I gladly replaced what dishes I had borrowed—no more than half, I'm sure—out of gratitude for the way God had changed my own circumstances."

"You should have told me."

She shook her head. "No. Like I said, I've been there. Not only would that have embarrassed you, I suspect you might have allowed pride to keep you from accepting what I wanted very much to give."

She was right, of course. Now, the least I can do is to pass her generous act along.

I hope I can remember that the next time my gangly young descendants knock the petals off my dried rose arrangement while playing sock 'em with the sofa pillows.

Lord, thank you for showing me the true meaning of friendship. Help me to go and do likewise.

Chapter 30

"Guarding" Angels

He will command his angels concerning you to guard you in all your ways.

—Psalm 91:11, NIV

Rain lashed relentlessly against my face and I could barely see to find our car as I crossed yet another new-to-us church parking lot with our two youngest children dripping along beside me.

"I'd loan you my umbrella but it's home in the closet," a cheery voice called as a hurrying young stranger splashed past and disappeared into the darkness.

For once the girls didn't argue for position as I unlocked and yanked open our car door. With our ninth grader beside me, and our lively first grader in the back seat, I maneuvered our old red station wagon into a straggling line of departing cars. Some friendly teenagers had invited the older girls to go for soft drinks and would bring them home later.

Two buses with doors yawning rumbled in front of the church, awaiting the last of their passengers.

Scrubbing steam from a back window with her coat sleeve, Renee complained, "I wish I was old enough to go get pop."

The atmosphere inside the church had been warm and friendly. Now, as I turned onto the street and maneuvered into the proper lane, the bereft feelings of a frequent mover crept in along with the dampness, and I knew the children too must feel lonely.

"Someday you will be," I assured her.

Rain lashed hard against the windshield and wipers slapped briskly as I braked for the stop sign a block from the church. Looking both ways, peering closely into twin tunnels of rain-drenched darkness formed by the cross street, I drove cautiously into the intersection.

"That car's going to hit us!"

The frightened child who screamed that warning is as certain today as then that the lights of the approaching car came on barely an instant before that red Pontiac Firebird slammed into us broadside.

"At least the scratches will match," I remember thinking as I heard in the silence the tinkling of broken glass. Then, shifting from the ridiculous, seeing that both children were all right, I whispered, "Thank you, Lord."

On impact, thanks to wet pavement, our heavier car had spun almost full circle. While our first grader got out of bed next morning wearing a shiner worth bragging about, her black eye and a small bump from tumbling against a window crank turned out to be the extent of our physical injuries.

While we waited through police procedure, church folks peered through steamy windows as the two buses drove past. Inside some of the cars an officer beckoned one at a time through the intersection were people with whom I had just shared a Bible study. No one, of course, knew our car. Not one person recognized us.

Finally, questions ceased and measuring came to an end. While our insurance company would call the car "totaled," the trusty vehicle-turned-junk-heap still ran. Bent frame, broken windows, caved-in side and all, if I could pull myself together, I had the officer's permission to drive what was left of it home.

By then, I could have used a good-sized bucket for collecting my own parts!

Breathing a prayer, I started the engine and drove down a wrong street in a strange town where street lights along broken or missing sidewalks seemed as scattered as my state of mind. While rain dittoed the Noah's day flood, I faked my way through the miserable streets as if I knew exactly where I was going. As I was about to return to the scene of the accident to try to recover my lost bearings, my seat partner looked first right, then left.

"Oh, yeah," Andie said, "this is the way the school bus takes; it's shorter."

Right.

At home, I moved zombie-like through bedtime routine, kissed the girls goodnight, and promptly fell the rest of the way apart. The teenagers came home too thrilled over the making of new friends to be bothered with Mom's silly little accident. Besides, there were lessons to be studied and outfits to be decided upon for morning. Next day, I realized I could have phoned and someone from that church would gladly have responded to my need. As it was, I shivered alone in a couch corner until after the two who had come in last had gone to sleep and the telephone rang.

"How was your day?" Norm asked from a motel room in Spokane.

At the sound of his steady voice, I burst into tears and blubbered so in the telling he could hardly make out what had happened. Blowing my nose, I described the accident again, this time more graphically. His level of sympathy remained at so-so (something we authors of fiction soon learn to expect).

At midnight, I was still awake and trying to still my shaking hands enough to read about other folks' problems in the evening paper when the small one crept quietly out to stand beside my chair.

"Remember? You told us in Bible club about 'guarding' angels? Ours really, really had to guard us tonight, didn't they?" she said with a giggle before giving my shoulder a pat and padding back down the hall to her bed.

Given our same circumstances, none save a child could have been so lighthearted. Still, I had to smile, for she was right. God *had* been with us. Even while I'd been deciding we couldn't possibly get home from there, he had helped us to find a right road by allowing us to take a wrong street.

In the middle of a dilemma, who besides God would have been so creative?

"Guarding" Angels

Lord, hold steady today those who, for whatever reason, find themselves all alone in an unfamiliar place faced with dilemma. Surround them with "guarding" angels and give clear direction to what may seem like extra scary paths.

It being Saturday, we were all busy with chores. The lawn had been mowed and the sprinklers were going.

"I should clean out the inside of that car, but it's so hot," the dad in our household remarked, referring to the company-owned car parked to one side in our driveway.

An hour or so later, he glanced out the window and saw water running from beneath the car's doors. Inside, on the floor back of the front seat, sat a small but turned-on sprinkler.

The small one had decided to help clean the car's interior—her way.

Needless to say, heat or no heat, the car got cleaned *and* dried—and dried—and dried some more.

Chapter 31

Mercy? Me?

Pleasant words are a honeycomb, sweet to the soul and healing to the bones.

—Proverbs 16:24, NIV

"When can we get the stuff for our 4-H outfits?"

This was not the first day our sixth grader had asked. Neither was it the first week. The truth was if a longsuffering 4-H leader was ever to teach Jennifer and Kristin to sew (with my grateful and exuberant blessing), then I must find a way to stretch our already strained budget and purchase needed supplies.

Conditioned throughout my own childhood years to consider money matters for adults only (a notion long-since trashed), I dismissed the two with a noncommittal "As soon as I find time to shop."

Two paydays passed before "time to shop" at last squeaked onto my list of weekly necessities. By then, the due date for the finished two-piece garments loomed frustratingly close.

That first exciting day, the girls cut, pinned, pressed, and took turns with the cantankerous portable sewing machine occupying one side of the kitchen table.

"I hope we get done today," our seventh grader said over a mouthful of peanut butter spread between slices of day-old bread as we lunched cross-legged on the floor.

"Cinchy," said her optimistic younger sister.

I shook my head. For starters, the projects were theirs to do. While I could encourage, demonstrate, explain, advise, and even sympathize, I could not offer to snip or to sew so much as a thread.

"Handwork takes time. You'll have to get with it," I warned that first day.

Due to school, homework, volleyball practice, Bible club, church, and who-knows-what-all, neither one got around to finishing the machine work until two Saturdays later. By then, enthusiasm had worn thin and I had started to nag.

"You can hang on the phone *after* you've finished your project."

"The minute your homework is done, you know what you need to do."

"If that skirt's not hemmed on time, it's not going to be my fault."

"Put that book away, and..."

To an experienced seamstress, the handwork looked simple: sew on a few buttons, hem blouse tail and sleeves, whip-stitch back side of skirt band, measure length and hand-hem skirt—a quick hop for this mom; a giant hurdle for beginners.

Still, "You are going to finish this handwork before you go to bed and that's that," I said over dessert the night before the projects were due. Having made senior high sewing class history with repeated ripping-out and re-doings, I now find it hard to believe I could even have considered issuing such a firm and ridiculous ultimatum.

Neither can I understand how a thinking mom could possibly have expected haste to take place under the lash of negative rhetoric. Not, "What beautiful, even stitches," but "Those stitches look like hula hoops for a circus fat lady!"

Or, "Buttons need to be able to wiggle. See how nicely these work on the front of your shirt," but, "You'll never get those buttonholes to lie flat over the buttons if you don't stop yanking your thread so tight."

"It's eleven o'clock—way past our bedtime," Kris ventured to suggest at one point.

"You're forever begging to stay up later; now's your chance," I retorted.

"I didn't mean this late," she said, yawning and digging at her eyes with the back of a fist cramped by unaccustomed needle maneuvers.

Unrelenting, yet trying to insert kindness into what I realized had become terse instructions, I stayed with them through the last saliva-stiffened knot.

"You're tired now, but you'll be proud of yourselves in the morning," I said at 12:35 A.M. as we folded the finished garments and laid them aside to be pressed the next day.

"You will maybe," Jennifer muttered as the two stumbled off to bed.

Next day, when we delivered the finished projects, the 4-H leader said with surprise, "No one ever gets them in on time. But that's OK," she hastened to add. "I'll keep these in the spare bedroom until the rest get theirs finished."

I bit my tongue to keep from exploding right there on her doorstep, then simmered over the matter for days. Why set a deadline if there was to be no deadline?

The girls? Having finished their projects, they went nonchalantly on to other things.

Along about then, it began to sink into my numb-from-nagging skull that self-discipline, like other virtues, is better caught than taught. Forced labor coupled with my desire for them to excel had probably produced no more than a duet of negative vibes on the subject of hand sewing.

Further, while blue ribbons got pinned to both outfits at the county fair that fall, and those matching skirts and blouses later became favorites, neither kid asked to sign up for 4-H the next year.

Lord, someone has said that it takes nine positives to erase a single negative. If that is so, then I am in debt clear up to my ears! Please, Lord, now that I have learned the value of being more positive, could you erase a few of the negatives that must surely remain like dark clouds among the memories of our children?

Chapter 32

Pain Gain

God made him who had no sin to be sin for us, so that in him we might become the righteousness of God.

—2 Corinthians 5:21, NIV

Tea parties are as integral to an all-girl family as are reeking sneakers to folks blessed with boys. In fact, if every peanut butter concoction this mom ever created could be interspersed with toothpick skewered carrot wheels and raisins, and placed end-to-end, the resulting kid-style smorgasbord would feed a small, small world and then some.

Tea sets can be found in assorted shapes and sizes. They may be breakable, unbreakable, exquisite, or cheap. The tea set that appeared beneath our tree that never-to-be-forgotten Christmas was neither priceless nor pretty; it was disturbingly useful.

A caution we learned early on in the multi-faceted business of growing children is that "useful" is not the way to go with an active four-year-old. Aware that the giver of the gift in question knew little of our child's determined ways, I breathed a silent prayer, "Lord, while you're blessing the beasts and children, do include Patsy. And, if you don't mind, please stick with her the next time she shops for our children, for she knows not what she is doing."

Our small person examined the full-color photo display covering the top and all four sides of the tea set box, undid the plastic wire securing a shiny replica of a percolator, and announced, "I can make real coffee."

Basking beneath tinsel and Christmas joy multiplied by seven, I murmured a noncommittal, "We'll see," as we continued with our unwrapping and exclaiming.

The father of these moppets and I had folded and tabbed and added the last cardboard deck chair to a Tammy doll house around 2 A.M. and awakened to the patter of ten tiny feet before six. After the last package had been opened, with dinner still hours away, we took advantage of what seemed a perfect opportunity to recoup, and collapsed into our cushiony corners while the kids played with their loot.

The minute the parents of an inventive preschooler close all four eyes simultaneously, it is a sure sign wisdom has eloped with common sense. To so relax while older siblings have their minds on collecting $200 whenever they pass Go smacks of stupidity.

Our first clue that all was not calm and neither was it bright, came in the form of high decibel, preschool type screeching, interspersed with the moans of a wounded fourth grader.

Renee had learned as a toddler never to touch the stove. Now that she was old enough to know better, she had located coffee, filled her new percolator with water, pushed a chair up to the stove, and turned on the fast-heat burner. The coffee soon sizzled over, creating a disagreeable odor that traveled all the way to the girls' bedroom and wafted down into Tammy's cardboard kitchen.

As the smell hit the sensitive nose of our blonde one, Andie dropped Tammy beside an imaginary pot of her favorite chicken noodle soup and ran to the real kitchen. Forgetting to grab a potholder, she snatched the toy pot from a red-hot burner, splashing coffee over a hand quickly seared by the pot's aluminum handle.

"I was making coffee for you guys 'cause you were tired," our budding chef explained on her way to a ten-minute "sit." "Besides," she defended, "you didn't say I couldn't make coffee. You said, 'We'll see.'"

Right. Just like I'd agreed Rudolph might need a long extension cord to plug in his nose.

Still, she never messed with the stove again.

The lesson reinforced by her sister, however, was of far greater value.

"I'm glad it was me who got burned and not her," Andie said before the pain in her burned hand could possibly have subsided.

Sometime during her few years of Bible stories and Sunday school, our nine-year-old had caught onto the love principle so graphically demonstrated by our Lord Jesus Christ as he bore the pain of the cross, paying the penalty for your sin and mine.

What a Savior!
Matter of fact, what a daughter!

Thank you, Lord, for each of those times when a child of ours (and yours) has caught the essence of what it means to be like Jesus.

On the subject of Christmas trees:

"The tree at church is really beautiful. We gots to have a fake tree 'cause Mom's "hallergical" to real trees. They give her the hiccups or something."

Chapter 33

Fair Game

Whoever listens to me will live in safety and be at ease, without fear of harm.

—Proverbs 1:33, NIV

Taking two kids to the county fair with hardly any money in your pockets is the pits. Double the pits once you hit the midway and must drastically limit the number of rides—pits that deepen as you brush past a pink cloud of sugary cotton candy and sniff the aroma of a little boy's corn dog. Hungry or not, you drool along with your offspring as you weave past booths offering a tantalizing array of the kinds of junk foods kids so love to smear over their fronts and faces.

The dilemma began when the older kids, who had their own money and had gotten to go to the fair with their friends, sounded forth at the breakfast table until the suffering on the face of their fourth grade sister got to be more than this perpetually broke mother could bear. Besides, a business friend had given us four free gate tickets. Money or no money, we might as well use them.

Since a free perusal of exhibit buildings and 4-H barns does not spell FAIR to children, I scraped the bottom of our fun money jar, added a wrinkled pair of grocery dollars, and issued instructions: "You will have to make choices. Three rides each and that's all, and one treat. One."

While choosing proved difficult and took time, our ten-year-old had been blessed with financial understanding long before her time. To not have money for something meant precisely that. To argue got you nowhere. To whine or throw a hissy fit meant you might as well head for the car.

A penny found on the sidewalk being big money to our youngest, she had not yet learned to deal with such family absolutes. Since she seldom got to go anyplace other than church and a few school functions, many of the no-money woes her siblings had learned to take for granted were still mystery to her.

At the fair, the treat part was easy. One giant dip of chocolate ice cream on a crunchy sugar cone and a taste of her sister's cotton candy and the small one was satisfied. Leading her through a maze of brightly lighted carnival rides was not.

After the way of all wise parents, we began our fair outing with a slow stroll through barns and exhibits of interest to children. This, of course, cut dramatically into time that might otherwise have been spent hustling kids past spinning lights and midway hawkers. The big flaw in the plan, as we realized later, was that treats and rides happened precariously close to bedtime. Missed bedtime for a preschooler accustomed to few sweets—none at all in the evening—and pajamas at eight, we well knew, could spell disaster in audible neon.

After exercising all the individual patience we possessed, borrowing at times from each other, my beloved and I finally managed to coax the small one on and off three rides of her own choosing and were headed on weary feet for the gate and the car when she spied the Ferris wheel. Not a little Ferris wheel centered among the kiddy rides, but the big one.

To understand what happened next, one must first realize that this granddaddy of all the Ferris wheels this young mom had ever laid eyes on above any fairgrounds ever was a thing of beauty. I had only to close my eyes to bring back butterflies of delicious remembrance having to do with my own long love affair with the Ferris wheel—whatever its size or the condition of its splendor. Lost in reverie, I only half-heard the pleas of our fifth-born.

"I want to go on the Ferris wheel.

"Please, Daddy? Please, may I?

"I never ever got to ride on the Ferris wheel. Please?

"Everybody else gots to ride on the Ferris wheel. Why can't I?"

As we stopped and gaped up at the brightly lighted wheel towering against a night sky, if she heard any response at all to her plea, it had to come from her father, for I too wanted in the worst way to ride on that Ferris wheel.

Why not? I reasoned, fingering the grocery dollars still in my pocket. Then, turning to her sister, I made what for me at the moment meant supreme sacrifice, "Do you want to go with her?"

While I could see the shine in our ten-year-old's eyes at the thought of a fourth and unexpected ride, she hung onto her dignity by saying, "She's going to have to shut up if I do."

The man to whom I am married does not do well in high places. He rode on the Ferris wheel once. He has no plans ever to do so again. There was no way he was going to understand how I could give in so easily to the whining of a four-year-old when it was already long past her bedtime.

While the man in charge of both levers and tickets waited with outstretched hand, I hung onto the eager one and shouted above the roar of the motor, giving instructions.

"Stay sitting down and mind your sister," I added between cupped hands after the precious dollars had been delivered and the two sat locked behind a bar that seemed suddenly flimsy protection for such young and fragile goods.

A shifting of gears and the Ferris wheel began to move. We saw the small one giggling and could tell by her body language that this was not her usual happy giggle but a nervous one. By the time most seats were full, and the seat holding our two had ascended over the top and begun its descent, the giggle looked more like a whimper.

"I want off," I distinctly heard her say to the operator after all seats were full and the Ferris wheel started to gain momentum.

"You're fine," he called as the seat moved upward.

She began to holler.

I stepped closer. "Maybe you'd better let her off," I suggested somewhere near the top of my lungs.

He shook his head and stepped back from the gears, allowing the Ferris wheel to turn at set speed.

The hollering turned into angry screeching.

I asked again.

"'T ain't fair to other customers," he said. "Besides, it costs money to be always stoppin' and startin'."

As screeching turned into wails of anguish, her sister let go of the bar with one hand and reached to embrace her. Rejecting the comforting arm in favor of added decibels, the small one squalled louder.

"Please, sir—"

"Look, lady. I stood right here and watched while that young miss begged and bawled till she got her way. Now I'm givin' it to her and she's not likin' it. But she ain't gonna learn if we cater to 'er caterwaulin'. Besides, she's not hurtin', she's just yellin'. I've seen it a million times—let 'er off an', dollars to donuts, she'll beg for another go-around." Pausing briefly, he added, "If'n it's any comfort to you, ma'am, I've run this thing with nary an accident since before you was born."

Giving up, I put my hands over my ears for the rest of a ride I know for certain ran twice as long as had the ride preceding it.

The minute our small one got off, she stomped her foot at the operator. "Why didn't you stop when I said?"

He looked her calmly in the eye. "Because you wanted t' ride. I heard you say so an' I heard you holler so, 'an not jus' once. So a ride you got. Now you git yourself over there and say 'thank you' to your mamma and daddy for spendin' their money and lettin' you ride. An' say it loud enough so's I can hear, you hear me?"

Without another word, she obeyed.

Two days later, she looked up from her bowl of Cheerios and announced, "Riding on the Ferris wheel was fun, wasn't it, Andie? Thanks, Dad. Thanks, Mom."

I smiled, thinking how interesting that she could so quickly forget the trauma of being left to stew in the juice of her own loud demands. Recognizing that "me too" had been involved in that Ferris wheel fiasco, my smile faded. Remembering the wise words and careful hands of the experienced operator who had kept our little one safe, now seemed a good time to pause and thank God for the safety net He provides while we bawl and complain over the inevitable consequences of our own poor choices.

Lord, we are sometimes surprised by how little time it takes for a child to change action or attitude following correction. Please teach me to respond in like manner to those disciplines that come from your hand.

Chapter 34

Game Plan

Guard what has been entrusted to your care.

—1 Timothy 6:20, NIV

Her father and I grinned at each other the day the athletic one bounced in after school and announced that she had signed on to play football for the annual powder puff game. Part tomboy, and a fast runner, Kris was also a scrapper. In our biased and football illiterate opinions, the team (a descriptive term open for debate) was lucky to get her.

Game day dawned bright and as clear as my Saturday schedule. Nothing, not even the chore list shifted to Saturday evening, was going to keep this mom from hollering her hardest at that game. Nothing, that is, except a pair of unexpected visitors we barely knew.

When the doorbell rang around 11 A.M., and a couple with whom we had once shared a table at a company function, and to whom we had issued a perfunctory "come see us some time," stepped across our threshold, I remember thinking how glad I was that they had arrived three hours before game time.

At 12:30, I cranked up my good manners and said, "Why don't I make us some sandwiches?" Perhaps the invitation would serve as a hint.

The moment those folks murmured, "That would be nice," I started to feel uneasy.

Over slapped-together sandwiches and a plate of cookies, feeling considerably less casual than my words must have sounded, I announced, "Our daughter is playing powder puff football this afternoon at 2 o'clock."

"Is that kind of like the touch football the Kennedy family plays?"

"No. It's regular football, but a shorter game with all girl teams."

"Oh," she said. "Did you do your wallpapering yourself?"

At 1:45, my tactful and blessed beloved asked, "Would you like to go to the game with us?"

They looked at each other, shrugged, and replied in unison, "Not particularly."

At that precise moment, I should have said, "Then I hope you won't mind if we leave you long enough to go. You're welcome to watch TV, look at a magazine, or whatever. We'll probably be back in less than two hours." I should have, but I didn't.

Instead, I silently prayed for their instant departure and patiently settled in for what turned out to be a long haul. Except for a not-too-subtle and constant glancing at his watch, Norm did likewise.

Because they did not leave until well past time for the game to have ended, the best I could say at the end of the day was, "At least they didn't hang around for supper."

We got the story over potato soup with cheese biscuits less than an hour after they had gone.

"Mom, you should have seen the cheerleaders. Those guys had on pleated skirts. Hardly any of them fit. One guy almost lost his."

"I could relate to him," said the one who had played the game. "We wore the guys' football uniforms and they gave me the smallest one and it nearly fell off several times."

"The game? How was the game?" I asked.

"Mom, you would have died laughing."

"I wish I had been there to at least try," I said.

Pointing at Kris, Jennifer said, "She had the ball. She could easily have made a touchdown—she was that close—but not Dumbo here, not my little sister. She had to do things her way."

By now they were all laughing so hard we probably could not have understood even if any one of them had stopped giggling long enough to speak.

"We'd laugh too if you could quiet down long enough to tell us what's funny," their father suggested.

"She—" Another burst of laughter. "She had the ball and she had her chance and she ran the wrong way."

"She made the only touchdown."

"For the other team!"

The one guilty of such dastardly play was laughing as hard as the rest. "The other girls on my team chased me all the way down the field trying to get me to turn around," she said between giggles.

"The coach about died."

"And I am sitting here dying because we missed it," I said.

"One teacher said this was our school's most historical game ever."

"You mean *hys*terical."

Yes, we missed a great game. What's more, later on in life, we were not always there when some from our all-girl household temporarily turned their backs on family goalposts or veered carelessly away even from game plans they had set for themselves. Unlike the hilarity sparked by that never-to-be-forgotten powder puff football game, there is nothing funny about it when kids forget what they've been taught, digress from the Way, and mess up their lives.

Still, while unforeseen circumstances kept us from watching that game of all games, in the end, we were there to laugh with our daughters. When they mess up, however, no drop-in guests or anything else should keep a parent from being there when a child needs a shoulder, not to giggle, but to cry on.

Lord, thank you for being our companion and our comforter. You are always there—to laugh with us, cry with us, and simply to be with us. Thank you, too, for all the pieces you have picked up in my life and in the lives of our children.

The value of marriage is not that adults produce children but that children produce adults. – *Peter De Vries*

Chapter 35

Sagebrush Saga

I have learned to be content whatever the circumstances... [because] I can do everything through him who gives me strength.

—Philippians 4:11b, 13, NIV

Warning: due to subject matter, the chapter you are about to read may get long. The verbosity to be found in a chapter, however, cannot begin to compare with the longest two weeks of family togetherness in the history of our combined seven lives.

In the first place, moving to a dusty little western Wyoming town surrounded by gas fields was no way to be spending our nineteenth wedding anniversary. Further, the one being transferred, the one writing this saga, and four out of our five kids had no desire to relocate. Given such a close proximity opportunity to bug her sisters, the one whose opinion counted least clambered as happily into our overstuffed car as if she were being driven to the mall.

As we left several hundred miles of semi-desert wasteland behind for more of the same, the disgruntled ones occupying the back seat hung crape over their sagging spirits in a minor key with a made-up song. To this day, I wish I had recorded those ninety-nine or so verses of *Way Out in the Middle of the Sagebrush*. Instead, while the clever words expressed my sentiments exactly, rather than write down or record the dirge, I sat like a lump and glumly scanned the horizon for more of what I believed to be the worst.

A house-hunting trip prior to transfer had turned up zilch. With no housing available, we resigned ourselves to the only option available and purchased a doublewide mobile home. The plan on the day following our arrival was that the vinyl-covered halves of said home were to be delivered to an assigned company housing lot, clinched together, weatherproofed, hooked up and made ready for occupancy.

"Not to worry," my transfer-weary spouse assured me. He had spoken specifically to the company office clerk about making reservations for us to spend a couple of nights in a motel at company expense.

Recalling the dreary cubbyhole in which we'd found ourselves during our house-hunting trip, I worried on.

Yes, he had made sure the fellow understood we must have sleeping space for seven.

What the lone male head of our otherwise female household had failed to observe was that the clerk, still in his early twenties, had never married and (we soon discovered) had no clue as to how many square feet of bed, bath, and closet it takes to keep five kids from kindergarten to college from killing each other. After passing a sign placing the population at 602—one glance at the town and we could tell the number was exaggerated—we pulled off onto a stretch of gravel in front of a low-slung motel in need of a paint job. Barely glancing at the room (singular) that had been reserved for us, we returned to the office and insisted, "There has to be a mistake!"

Not only had there been no mistake, the neon *No Vacancy* flashing before the only other motel in town meant exactly what it said. Unless some traveler or workman unfortunate enough to be holed up in such a forsaken place moved on, we were stuck.

Knowing the company stood good for whatever, the motel proprietor couldn't have cared less. In reply to some insistent carping, she finally offered a diffident, "We can set up a rollaway."

Kris, our middle child promptly put her dibs on the rollaway—never mind where we were going to unfold one if indeed such a contraption should be forthcoming. Following her lead, four kids staked out claims with four special pillows plopped onto the four sides of the two double beds.

As I was trying to decide how best to condense seven people, seven large and small suitcases, one full-to-bursting clothes bag, four cosmetic cases, one toy tote and a doubled grocery sack filled with games no one had gotten happy enough to play, Andie, now in fifth grader observed, "There aren't enough beds. Mom, I guess you and Dad will have to find someplace else to sleep."

Her neat disposal of the two who had brought her safely thus far instantly made getting started with a plan easier.

"Now I *know* who's sleeping on the floor."

Along with beds, the room's furnishings consisted of a desk and straight chair, and one small nightstand with lamp attached. Located between beds, the stand held one telephone and an eight-page (with names double-spaced) regional telephone directory. A short bar-and-shelf arrangement (presumed to be closet space) occupied the inner wall of a 5' x 5' ell at the bathroom end of the room. The vintage washbowl in the single-occupancy bathroom provided no hint as to where one might lay a toothbrush. Still, while the shower proved to be an elbow knocker, the bath was clean and its thin towels plentiful.

Setting up the rollaway beneath the now-loaded clothes rack left two inches of rollover space in the bed below, and fourteen inches for getting to the bathroom. With a little shoving, we eked space for two sleeping bags between beds and against one wall.

Contrary to plans and promises, the mobile home did not roll into town the next day; the moving van did. Due to the discrepancy, our worldly goods had to be dumped into a warehouse belonging to someone somebody knew, a kindness on the part of a stranger we would not easily forget.

First day of school outfits having been packed into four suitcases "just in case," and the iron included, the opening of school next day should have been cinchy. Instead, birth certificates and immunization records being required, and said papers having been packed by mistake in one of a jillion look-alike boxes marked "office," this mom had to show up at all three schools and beg for mercy before three principals.

There being no way a kid could risk entering a classroom wearing a rerun outfit, preparation for day two of school got worse. After unlocking the warehouse and rummaging through boxes and cardboard closets until all had a change, we had then to decide where to put still more stuff.

By the end of week one, a dad's tolerance for trivialities being somewhat lower than a mom's, it's hard to say who suffered most. Since Norm basked daily beneath the privilege of an eight-hour escape from this female dominated prison, and had only to make it to the head of the line for time and space in which to shave and dress, I thought I knew.

"Walk to the library," I snapped the first time our senior high duo complained of having no place to study.

"There isn't any."

I should have known. Not in a town where they counted population over a twenty-mile radius and included pipeline mileposts in the count.

"If I flunk math, it's because of this dumb light," our sophomore grumbled.

"Pretend it's a birthday candle or go sit on the step." I had problems of my own.

Two skirts plus a dress I'd been making for an opening reception were yet to be finished before the usually cheerful one departed for college three days hence. The ironing board having already been installed across the foot of the rollaway, we returned to the warehouse for my sewing machine and the card table. Once the card table was in place (the only place), to get to the bathroom meant you either had to crawl across both beds or tunnel beneath the table and risk tangling with electrical cords and/or Mom's foot. While sewing clothing in the midst of such chaos bordered on crazy, keeping busy made it easier for me to handle mealtimes and all the rest that was going on.

Three meals a day for two solid weeks, we straggled across the street to order meals having not the slightest resemblance to Mom's or even Dad's home cooking. Faced with certain of those culinary disasters, I was tempted to rebel along with our five-year-old.

Latching onto the fact that neither parent appeared likely to create a scene, not even in the most remote corner of a busy restaurant, said five-year-old refused either to eat or to order anything other than "scottage cheese" and hot chocolate.

Since half-days in kindergarten did not include lunch, the sketchy diet soon gave cause for concern. Assigned to the only table big enough for our brood, a creative waitress, a mother to six, took over.

The next time we ordered, she brought the usual cup of hot chocolate along with the rest of our beverages. When she returned with entrees, however, the mound of cottage cheese she plunked before the wide-eyed picky one resembled a small formal garden. Bordered by a carrot-stick-and-celery fence, a handful of toothpick stems held assorted fruit bites so tastefully arranged our littlest rebel could not resist. From that day forward, she ordered "scottage cheese" with "toothpicks 'n' stuff."

The day our house finally arrived, its two halves had to be backed into a narrow spot and connected. After two days of cussing (not I—the trailer haulers) and hammering, we collected our belongings from warehouse and motel and moved home.

Next morning, after my spouse and the tall and helpful one had escaped over the Wyoming border into Idaho with the finished clothes, a pile of luggage, and our college-bound eldest, I ran across the two boxes of Bartlett pears I had optimistically assumed I would long-since have had time to can.

To continue with the comedy of errors that took place over the next seventeen months would confirm what we soon came to know. During our stay in a town not one of us ever came to love, we all started to learn to be content, not only in the State of Wyoming, but in all those other states to which we were later transferred.

Further, while giving birth was about all I got spared during our stay in that motel, I think I better understand the dilemma faced by Joseph and Mary after they traveled all the way to Bethlehem and found no room in the inn.

Some in the family even got a little taste of how Jesus must have felt, having no place to lay his head.

Father, as I struggled with a third rewrite and the length of this chapter, you reminded me of the countless families worldwide who live in a single room day in and day out. Thank you for the privileges we enjoy in our country. Thank you, too, for supplying the grace that got us through those two weeks!

Chapter 36

Wing Ding

Cast all your anxiety on him because he cares for you.
—1 Peter 5:7, NIV

Sending our firstborn off to college hit this mom's panic button considerably harder than had releasing her to face the wide, wide world on her first day of school. While we found comfort in knowing she had chosen a Christian college in the state bordering ours, as with other firsts, the misery that hit during the process of Anita's departure from home can only be described as the pits.

Why? Because for however many years it takes for a kid to make it from kindergarten through commencement, like the daily newspaper, that child will continue to show up on your doorstep. Not always on time perhaps, but she *will* come home. She will turn up her freckled nose at the food on your table, take over the family bathroom, squabble with siblings, and demand a fair share of the dollars allotted for new clothes.

But the day a nearly grown child flies from the nest and heads for college, that's it. You've had your say: she is now on her own (scary) and will be making her own decisions (even scarier). What's more, her choices may not always be the best (scariest of all).

Due to circumstances beyond anyone's control, the trauma connected with saying goodbye to the cheerful one got inflated. Two weeks prior to freshman orientation, we moved about as close to the ends of the earth as one can get and still remain in the USA. (The best—not much—and the worst having to do with that unwanted transfer ground out more grist than this author could possibly cram into even a lengthy chapter, a chapter you will find elsewhere in this book.) For the college-bound, while she was now free to make her own choices, that long-distance move meant she no longer had a familiar house or room, or even friends, to which and to whom she could return.

Too, I had always expected to be there for her on the day she moved into the dorm. We would hang curtains together, put her things away, and enjoy one last mother-daughter talk. At noon, we might visit over hamburgers at the student center with her roommate and *her* mother. Our little freshman would wave across the room at one of her dorm mates. Reassured that she was among friends, I could go home and start trying to squeeze the cost of long distance calls into what, for years to come, proved to be a tuition-stressed budget.

Now that we had moved, there was no way anything remotely resembling the above could happen. Not with clothes and school paraphernalia to be assembled in time for her four sisters to be properly attired and equipped for classes on Monday morning.

Still hoping, I said to the father of this brood, "You'll need someone to help drive, especially coming home." Considering the long and sometimes cattle or antelope-blocked drive from Big Piney, Wyoming across most of Idaho and a projected dozen or more trips up three flights of stairs carrying her stuff, the 450-mile return trip was sure to be tiresome.

Viewing her sister's trip to school as an opportunity to try out a newly acquired driver's permit, Jennifer said, "I'll go."

While hers was the only possible solution, Friday's goodbye will forever remain high on the list of all the goodbyes this mom has ever had to say. As for the one who was leaving, outwardly at least, her goodbye might well have been translated, "good riddance." After all, she would soon be free of parental intervention and be her own boss. After praying for God's protection, I waved until they were out of sight, and bawled when no one was looking.

The dad in this story being due back at work on Monday, and his driving partner for her first day in a new school, he had said before leaving, "We won't take time to attend church Sunday morning. With good driving conditions, we might possibly make it back home in time for the evening service."

They didn't. The rest of us went, came home, made popcorn, and guzzled hot chocolate. At 9:00, I shooed the older girls off to bed, tucked the small one in, and tried to read.

They should have been here long before now.

Turning on the 10 o'clock news, I listened for accident reports.

Where can they be?

Maybe they got a late start.

Perhaps they decided to attend church after all.

Should I call the highway patrol?

A little past midnight our red Ford station wagon finally crunched onto the narrow strip of gravel beside the front step of our newly acquired mobile home. One glance at their weary faces, and I knew something had gone awry.

"What's wrong?" I asked the tall one, the one with traces of tears marking an uncommonly ashen complexion

"A sage hen flew up in front of us," said her dad. "It was late dusk—getting pretty dark—it hit the windshield."

"It almost hit me," Jennifer said, her voice trembling.

"You mean it broke the windshield?"

"Sailed right between our heads and landed clear in the back. Never touched either of us. She was a big one, evidently been fattening herself up for winter. You might want to look at those glass cuts. You know what it's like across there—there's no place to stop."

As we moved to the light, tiny shards of glass glistened in Jennifer's hair. Miraculously, only a few small cuts dotted her upper chest.

"We couldn't travel fast, not with air whistling through that big hole in the windshield," my husband said. "That sagebrush desert gets mighty cold after dark."

To shorten the distance, they had left the freeway and taken a secondary road. Knowing my spouse, I suspect he may have stretched the speed limit a little. However, at 55 mph or even less, a sage hen could easily have become a lethal weapon. What if one or both of them had been hit?

"We prayed for God's protection. We needed it for sure," said the injured one. She smiled a weak smile. "God answered our prayers. I don't know what my face would look like if he hadn't."

Along about then, something much bigger than a sage hen struck me. Could not the same God who had diverted the flight of a fat feathered sage hen also look after the child now trying her wings 500 miles away at college?

To make a four-year-long story short, he could, and he did.

Father, help me to grow strong in the areas of faith and trust. Let me rest in the assurance that your hand is strong and mighty to deliver and that you are always present with each of your children. Thank you once more for maneuvering the flight pattern of an old sage hen and for lending your voice to the choices made by our firstborn, our lastborn, and those in between—whether they listen or not.

Overheard during a second grade brag session: "Well, my dad can take a whole car apart and put it back together again, and it even runs."

Chapter 37

Heart Smart

Do not be anxious about anything, but in everything, by prayer and petition, with thanksgiving, present your requests to God.

—Philippians 4:6, NIV

The Valentine banquet promised to be a big affair. If you didn't believe it (and who among the thirty-some people worshipping together in that struggling little church in Big Piney, Wyoming possibly could), all you had to do was ask any one of an overly optimistic youth group. Those five girls and three boys had freely and fervently discussed the matter and come up with a plan. They would divide up names, go at it one-on-one and, before the week ended, invite the entire senior high student body. If no one else among the 100 or so students agreed to come, all eight figured they could count on their friends.

The kids put feet to their prayers, solicited cooks and servers, asked for food donations, and begged the church board to please foot the rest of the bill.

"We'll need a humongous turkey, maybe two," said our third born.

I hadn't the heart to tell her. Having been in small churches all our lives (the Big Piney church being one of the smallest), I had either served or been served at a dozen struggling church Valentine banquets. The success rate for outreach, and sometimes for in reach had so often proved dismal, my heart ached daily for the young people and a plan that was certain to bring deep disappointment.

Added to the fact that hardly any of the 602 ranchers, cowhands, gas-field employees, and children living within a twenty-mile radius attended either our church or any other of three equally tiny churches, or exhibited any interest in doing so, we had no speaker. The kids couldn't even come up with a person willing to stand up and tell a good joke.

A week prior to the banquet, after just one for-sure ticket had been given away, I suggested, "Perhaps a smaller turkey will do."

The tall one gave me a look. "Mom, we're praying about it."

So was I—along with four other concerned moms and the rest of the church.

My food contributions to the banquet included twice-baked potatoes (cinchy for twelve to fifteen at the most) and a Christmas salad (a red-white-and-green gelatin and cream cheese concoction many in our family would die for) large enough to fill my biggest glass pan. I had also agreed to write and to read something both light and laughable for the young people (not at all cinchy since kids don't necessarily agree with parents on the subject of funny).

Having in mind that our big family would make short work of the thirty-five to forty pounds sure to be left, I purchased a fifty-pound bag of potatoes. The recipe being generous, the two salads turned into three. No problem. I had agreed with the other ladies that we should prepare plenty of food just in case. Besides, an extra salad would do for a start toward feeding the guests we nearly always invited for Sunday dinner. Should the banquet leftovers turn into a biblical and brimming twelve baskets, we could always announce a church potluck.

By the last Tuesday prior to banquet date, the kids had managed to give away six fairly positive tickets and a "maybe." The pastor, who openly admitted to a lack of teen rapport, had reluctantly agreed to say something. Leaving plenty of elbowroom, fifteen (if indeed that many showed up) would fill two tables.

Then came Wednesday, and the girls burst through the front door after school as if dogged by the boogieman.

"Mom!" the two hollered at once. "You'll never guess who spoke in assembly!"

National School Assembly speakers were especially popular in our tiny town, a town in which both main street and sidewalks got rolled up at dusk, and where little happened that was fun for kids.

"I couldn't."

"Tex Yearout!"

"You're kidding! I didn't even know he did school assemblies." In Washington, where we had once lived, Tex had served as Youth for Christ director. We had heard him often. He was a kids' kind of speaker if ever there was one.

"Did the students like him?" I asked, at the same time wondering how such an outspoken Christian (albeit a funny one) could get by with speaking in public schools.

"They loved him!"

The question that followed hit like a ton-sized snowball on a hot day in July, broke into bits, and immediately started to melt.

"Mom, do you think we could get him to speak at our banquet?"

Hedging, I said, "He probably has an agenda."

"He's going to Salt Lake City from here."

"There are lots of high schools in Salt Lake City," I warned.

"But the banquet is Friday night. They *never* plan assemblies for Friday night," Kris reminded me.

"Could we ask him?"

"Do you know where he is staying?" Silly question. Wyoming winters are never to be toyed with and the road to Salt Lake City passed through steep mountains. Having spoken for assembly late in the day, it seemed almost certain he would have waited until morning to make that drive. There were but two motels in town and one of them was almost always filled with regulars.

"Mom, would you call and ask him, pleeeeeease?"

"Why don't you call him?"

"I'm too chicken."

Reluctantly, foreseeing an answer I knew neither of the girls wanted to hear, I opened the phone book and dialed the motel. Tex Yearout's answer was gracious but final, "Sorry. Thanks for asking. I really can't."

Holding the receiver, seeing disappointment spread over the faces of our daughters, it was my turn to beg. "Mr. Yearout," I said, "have you any idea how hard it is to secure a Christian speaker of any kind in a place like this? If you'd heard our kids when they rushed in after school…" Having his ear, knowing he was a kind man, I went on for perhaps another two minutes, attempting to persuade him to come. He turned me down.

Since none of the boys claimed to be musical, the kids had agreed that our two girls would sing a duet and Jennifer, along with the pastor's two daughters, would form a trio. The fifth girl would ask the blessing and the oldest of the boys would offer the benediction. That, along with whatever the pastor found to say, and the reading I had not yet written, would be the program.

Attempting to write under the circumstances, however, turned into the ultimate of pits. The moment I put pen to paper, a lump moved in below where my tonsils used to be and I could think of nothing to say that anyone could possibly find amusing. So I dragged out that big bag, scrubbed twenty large potatoes and stirred gelatin into boiling water for the first step toward a three-layer salad.

That was Thursday morning. Thursday evening, the telephone rang.

"Tex Yearout, here," said a cheerful male voice. "I'll come. I've thought it over; I've prayed about it, and I'll come."

"I'll speak for the fun of it—no fee," he said in reply to my question. Having gone on to Salt Lake City, he added, "I'll speak for free, but I'll need travel expenses and a place to stay."

"You've got it," I said, knowing full well who had probably just been elected to plan details and pick up the tab.

Friday morning, the dimpled one phoned between classes to say, "So far, I've invited seventeen kids and they're all coming!"

At noon, after I had finished scooping and mashing potatoes from thirty-six carefully halved potato skins, I heard from the mother of one of the boys. "The kids compared notes at lunch and they've invited a total of eighty—they're all coming. He thinks by the end of the day, they'll have the whole school." By the time she had finished, I had turned the oven back on, dumped the rest of the potatoes in the sink, and started the cold water running.

Hysterical by the time the total reached 101 (counting the speaker) I quickly finished the piece I had been struggling to write but had no time to copy off potato smeared paper onto a clean sheet. At 6:20 (the banquet was at 7:00), I lifted the last cookie sheet filled with twice-baked potatoes from the oven. At the church, the boys had taken everything out of that tiny home mission church sanctuary, set up tables borrowed from the Catholics, and quickly turned the place into a banquet room. In the Sunday school rooms we were using for a kitchen, we cut all three glass pans of salad into small rectangles, lifted 101 pieces onto a generous bed of lettuce and slapped a canned pear half alongside to keep the stingy servings from looking skimpy. The lady in charge of cooking the meat cut up a couple of ready-cooked hams and added a generous slice alongside what would otherwise have been but slivers of turkey. Thanks to our one small grocery store, we had plenty of green beans plus their entire supply of rolls gotten in for the weekend. One heart-shaped cookie (instead of the two intended) on a red paper plate with some ice cream made a really pretty dessert.

The pastor switched roles, did a passable job as emcee, and the musical numbers went well. While I had not had a chance to take a shower, or even to don fresh makeup, my *Puppy Love* reading not only tickled a hundred teen funny bones, it drew cheers and whistles. When Tex Yearout stood, the kids broke into spontaneous applause that lasted through several attempts on his part to speak.

For more than an hour, he kept them listening and laughing and sobering every now and then to quietly listen to a spiritual application.

Did we see the beginnings of a great revival or even a flocking to church among those students? No. But let this mom be first to say that the smiles on the faces of a small group of teenagers who dared to trust God, and the generosity of a tired public speaker in the face of our need, made not only my day, but served as an encouragement to a whole lot of others.

Truth is, not one of the church ladies who helped seemed to mind that a few green beans floating in a pan next to a pile of empties meant our stomachs had to sit there and growl through a program not one person present was likely to forget.

More importantly, if those kids could trust God for an entire student body, and see him answer their prayers, I suspect that the same prayer-answering God can do more. He is quite capable, in fact, of seeing to it that 100 kids never quite forgot what Tex had to say about God's love, or about the banquet that filled up our hearts as well as our church.

Thank you, Lord, for the spirit of generosity on the part of one man and for whatever influence his kind act may have left on one small town. Bless him richly, Lord, and cause his tribe to increase!

Christmas Salad

Layer 1: 2 boxes cherry flavored gelatin. Mix as directed on box; pour into 9" × 12" pan or appropriate molds, and allow to set.

Layer 2: 2 c. boiling water
1 box lemon flavored gelatin
½ c. sugar
2 c. miniature marshmallows

Dissolve gelatin, sugar and marshmallows in boiling water. Cool and Add: ½ pint cream, whipped and mixed with:

1 8-ounce package cream cheese, moistened with hot water Pour slowly over set red gelatin and allow to set.

Layer 3:1 box lime gelatin. Mix as directed on box, cool, spoon carefully over lemon layer, allow to set. Serve in squares (this is also quite pretty when made in individual or in large molds).

Chapter 38

Bus Blunder

Bear with each other and forgive whatever grievances you may have against one another. Forgive as the Lord forgave you.

—Colossians 3:13, NIV

"Hurry up! If we miss the bus it's going to be all your fault!"

Thus began still one more first day in yet another new school. The sharp words spewing from the mouth of our usually gentle seventh grader served as a reminder. Our most recent move had happened much too close to the last. At our house, moving couldn't be helped. Given our breadwinner's profession, Mom had learned to shift with the territory. The kids had too, though seldom simultaneously.

For the parents of the two squabbling, the move had included a whopping answer to prayer. And, while the new schools were larger, and today might seem hard to the children, by tomorrow they would be fine. I said as much to the disgruntled one after our dawdling first grader at last buckled her red shoes and submitted to the dragging her sister, at the moment, considered appropriate for getting her out the front door.

"Mom, you don't know what it's like to be the dumb new kid with the stupid little sister."

"About like being Mom to a passel of crabby kids," I refrained from retorting.

Since no amount of faked good cheer was likely to sweeten her attitude, I pulled a smile out of cold storage and said, "Have a good day." That afternoon, in double declaratives, I learned exactly what it had been like to be a "dumb new kid with a stupid little sister." Blame, flung across the kitchen in escalating decibels, insisted that good old Mom was at fault for a mix up directly related to having switched schools.

The school switch had to do with our living for a short time outside city limits in the doublewide mobile home we had expected to sell before we moved. Since the transfer had come near the middle of the school year, and we planned to move into town as soon as the mobile home sold, we arranged for our first grader to attend Sand Hill Elementary in town rather than start her in the small country school where she would soon have to make another change. I expected to have to drive her to school each day. However, since her need for transportation would be limited to a few weeks, permission was given for her to ride the bus into town along with junior and senior high students.

The plan got off to a smooth start until an inexperienced office worker glanced at our small one's paperwork and, without bothering to check with anyone else, changed her enrollment from Sand Hill to Rosewood Elementary, located a few blocks away on the same street. With the small one beside me, I drove by Rosewood so she would know what her new school looked like. While we later learned that the placement error had to do with the medication our first grader happened to be taking at the time, no one had thought to inform her sister of the change.

I knew she was to go to Rosewood.

She knew she was to go to Rosewood.

Our seventh grader "knew" she was to go to Sand Hill. What's more, every junior high student riding the bus that morning knew something we, being new and uninformed, did not. Rosewood was the only school in town designated for special education. In the unthinking and often unkind language of those adolescents, Rosewood was a school for "retards."

Now, listening to the anguished garble bouncing off the walls of my busy kitchen, I at last pieced together what must have taken place.

"Creep" being her favorite current title of "endurement," I could almost hear the older one hiss, "Get off, you little creep," as the bus stopped before Sand Hill to let off one other student.

"It's not my school."

"It is too your school."

"No! My school is square. This school is rectangle."

Adding force to her half of the argument, the larger then grasped the arm of the smaller, propelling her off the bus and onto the step. There she clung until the bus driver produced a memo stating that the protesting one was indeed to be dropped off at Rosewood.

Had that bus been loaded with grade school kids, the sisterly tiff might have gone unnoticed. But we're talking junior high here—rude, immature, and a whole lot of it. They not only laughed, they hooted and hollered.

"Then," stormed the indignant one, "when they discovered the dumb new student's dumb little sister had to go to a school full of retards, I felt really dumb. I'm never ever going to ride that bus again!"

She did, of course, the very next morning. It took a while longer, however, for a school secretary to admit her mistake in moving our child's enrollment simply because she was on medication. By the time the principal got around to apologizing for failing to explain the special role assigned to Rosewood school, I too had all but stooped to name-calling.

Eventually, the small one got transferred back to the school where she belonged and our maturing one apologized for the name-calling. While she soon found new friends, she never did like that junior high very much. And she's never forgotten the day two new kids got labeled "dumb" through no fault of their own.

Crummy stuff like that happens to families and in life. Try as we might, as mere parents, we have no great solutions or power-packed erasers with which to magically wipe ugly memories off kids' sometimes indelible slates.

Still, when life hands one of us a bad rap (or a school secretary goofs), catching a mom or dad in the act of forgiving and forgetting can make those two exercises a lot easier for the offspring. What's more, even if it gets her laughed clear off the bus, every kid needs to know from the start, and believe with all her heart, that every student who was ever enrolled in a school such as Rosewood is as precious in God's sight as are those who go to schools like Sand Hill or hang out at the junior high.

Lord, make me an instrument of your peace as I try my best to model Christ for my children. Through their critical and candid observing of my behavior, may they know to love, respect, and show high regard for all people—even those who are different—both by their actions and in words they speak.

Chapter 39

Copycat

Be imitators of God, therefore, as dearly loved children and live a life of love, just as Christ loved us and gave himself up for us as a fragrant offering and sacrifice to God.

—Ephesians 5:1–2, NIV

With pets being as necessary to the rearing of children as peanut butter sandwiches and piano lessons, we've probably owned fewer than our fair share, but enough. Along with an ever-dying line of guppies and goldfish, we've given place to a fuzz ball baby chicken that cheeped non-stop for forty-two hours before we carried it back through the gate to a well-meaning neighbor. Since most of the places we've called home have been inside city limits and, in our country-kid hearts, we believe that man's best friend deserves more to explore than the wire mesh at the end of a ten-foot dog run, we've had cats, not the least visible of which was Twinkletoes.

Twinkletoes—so named because of four white feet attached to an otherwise black cat—joined our household in the midst of a move. While she was obviously too young to be separated from her mother, who belonged to a neighbor, it was either take her or leave her. Since the kids had grown attached and we were fresh out of cats, we took her. Unlike us who claim to be human, animal babies almost always behave like their own kind. Twinkletoes, we soon learned, was a crazy, mixed-up exception.

The new neighborhood turned out to be squirrel city. The bushy-tailed rodents chattered in trees and swarmed over our back yard like mothers at a garage sale.

At first, having survived early kitten-hood with milk from an eyedropper, Twinkletoes stalked the squirrels in typical beginner cat fashion. With her wee tail twitching, she would sneak across the grass on her plump belly and pounce toward the spot where a wily squirrel may or may not have been sitting.

The squirrels loved her baby games. Like parents doting over a toddler's first steps, they sat on their orange-brown haunches and discussed the newcomer in bursts of proud squirrel chatter. As the kitten grew older, their doting turned to teasing and eventually to what could only be described as play.

We thought nothing of it when Twinkletoes began walking the fence and shinnying face-first down the swing set chain. But when she started to cavort and meow in the midst of her bird stalking, she looked downright squirrely!

Fall came, and the squirrels rallied to the sound of walnuts rattling from our neighbor's two trees onto a shingled garage roof. Back and forth they scurried, collecting nuts and burying them beneath tree roots and throughout the yard.

One day I watched with disbelief as Twinkletoes extracted a single morsel of dry cat food from her dish, carried it into the yard and buried it, then repeated the ritual.

Cats are domestic animals. They do not store food, but depend on humans or a daily catch for their provisions. Having no feline parents to teach her, the now half-grown kitten had taken her instructions from our yard full of squirrels.

Come spring, she joined them in a dangerous (for copy cats at least) swinging game on the bushy ends of our highest elm tree limbs. That summer, she tight-roped over a nearby power line as easily as if she were walking to the mall.

Most of Twinkletoes' adventures proved harmless. The buried Kibbles, of course, did not survive the winter. She did not know, in fact, she should dig them up. And more than once when she got too high-minded, she thunked to the ground and walked off meowing to herself in disgruntled cat language. Eventually, she began acting more like a cat.

Imitating squirrels is all right for kittens, but the kids and we decided we would have a hard time swinging from a twig. Without special shoes and a whole lot of practice, there's no way any of us could make it across a power line.

For a family determined to follow Jesus, the Bible points not to squirrels or alternative lifestyles, but to Christ himself, and to godly men and women worth emulating. Could be that what gets interpreted as overprotection has less to do with parental control than with shielding children from danger and confusion until they grow old enough to deal with reality. Unlike Twinkletoes, kids do not have nine lives.

Lord, may the footsteps of Jesus form the very path our children will always choose to follow.

"Books are good friends," I said after lunch one hot day as I instructed our older children to choose a book and find a comfy spot in which to rest. "Taking a rest with a good friend is really special."

As I left the room, I heard our eight-year-old mutter, "What she means is reading a book on a hot day makes us shut up and go to sleep."

Chapter 40

We Always Laugh on Sunday

And whatever you do, whether in word or deed, do it all in the name of the Lord Jesus, giving thanks to God the Father through him.

—Colossians 3:17, NIV

Judging by leg count and decibels, some Sundays it looked as if this harried wife of a traveling husband might easily be the only mother in town cooking dinner. This was especially true during the years marked by triple PTA and tandem tuition, when friends and boyfriends swarmed over after church like gnats under a peach tree.

At the time, we owned eight matching plates, eight everyday assorted, and ten chairs. Stretched to the capacity of our modified, economized, country style kitchen, elbow to rib, our vintage table could accommodate twelve. Twelve, that is, if two agreed to go halvsies with the piano bench. Twin pullout bread boards coupled with mismatched stools and an apple box upturned before a gap vacated by a retired dishwasher made room for three more. Whenever guests added to our family of seven totaled more than fifteen, surplus diners either hunched over the living room coffee table or balanced plates on their laps.

This was one of those Sundays.

"Give the bread boards paper," I snapped when our junior high table-setter complained that she and the friend she'd brought from church had run out of plates.

In the living room, Norm struggled to keep awake as he read stories to Renee from her Sunday school paper while keeping an ear tuned to the high school duo occupying the arms of a couch sagging with shaggy-haired boys.

I glanced at the clock. In addition to her usual assortment of dorm mates, our oldest had invited her roommate's visiting mother and sister to dine with us. The peas boiled over, causing a stench and forming brown rings around the burners and a puddle on the floor, and the potatoes were yet to be mashed. If a hungry young buck nabbed two pieces, did my trusty electric skillet contain enough Swiss steak to go around?

I worried on. Should I seat the Canadian strangers facing stove and cabinet clutter that included a view of the pulled-out bread boards? Or would folks who without doubt took their meals in a more formal setting rather gawk into our door-less utility with its tangle of mops and brooms, coats and clothesbaskets? The piano bench sat opposite the only window, which offered the uninspiring and real life picture of a clumsy homemade swing set left behind (to the delight of our small one) by a previous owner.

Further, while my spouse and kids and guests had worshipped, I had committed a full hour-and-a-half to leading children's church.

"One of these days I'm going to resign from Sunday dinner," I groused, giving the potatoes what for.

Moments later, I slapped a gracious smile between my perspiring freckles and warmly greeted the rest of our guests. Somehow, we all found a plate and a place and I'd counted six more pieces of meat than plates.

Having roused and rallied to the done smell of food, my spouse had asked the blessing and was offering our Canadian guests first dibs at the meat platter when the little redhead from next door appeared outside our open window. Given permission to leave her stool long enough to speak with her friend, Renee told Jyme to "play on the swing set while you wait."

Her message delivered, she returned to her stool, then quickly ran back to the window.

"Don't worry if you hear us laughing," she called to Jyme. "We always laugh on Sunday."

While I had been burdened by place settings and spills and a lack of frills, our six-year-old had caught the essence of a day blessed with the togetherness of family and friends.

Needless to say, I've not yet gotten around to resigning from Sunday dinner.

Lord, while hospitality is not one of my gifts, with your help, I can learn to be hospitable. May our every guest be impressed, not with culinary or table setting finesse, but with the abiding presence of Christ who is the center of our home.

Chapter 41

Nit Picking

The seed that fell among thorns stands for those who hear, but as they go on their way they are choked by life's worries.

—Luke 8:14, NIV

"Yum. Chocolate chip. This is Traci," Renee, whose exuberance sometimes reminded us of a wiggly warm puppy, bounced in and announced one late September afternoon.

While the girls helped themselves to cookies, I welcomed this first time visitor, scraped the last of the dough from the bowl and (covertly, I hope) studied Traci.

Looking like a fizzled balloon beside our buoyant one, Traci, with her lackluster hair and dingy shorts outfit, was typical of the strays our budding Mother Teresa had befriended since kindergarten.

Other than being female and enrolled in the same junior high school, the two had little in common. While the simple clothing our child preferred took up less than half the space in her closet, even around the house, she was always clean about her person and attractively dressed. Soiled T-shirts and a distasteful blend of body odor and stale tobacco smoke were as much a part of Traci as were ripped sandals and chipped orange nail polish.

The dad in our lives had studied and worked hard to become a sought-after specialist in his field. Traci's father was an unemployed drunk whose idea of providing for a family began and ended with a broken down rental house beside a used car lot in an area zoned commercial. We all loved and served the Lord and went to church; Traci did not. Neither did she respond to Renee's repeated invitations.

For a time after the two went on to high school, it looked as if they might go their separate ways. Then one day, "I'm trading lockers," the one who boarded the bus from our house informed me.

Since there were no rules against trading, to trade was no big deal. Except that she and her current locker partner had been friends for so long, I had to ask.

"Can't you two get along?"

"It's not that—she understands—it's Traci. Mom, no one will share a locker with her. Some of the girls act awful to her."

While no mother in her right mind would likely have chosen Traci for a daughter's most desirable friend, I was proud of our offspring. Being Jesus to the unlovely took courage. What's more, Traci did not "filch and copy papers" or "steal our charitable one blind" as had been predicted by knowing classmates. Until that terrible Sunday before Thanksgiving, in fact, the locker arrangement appeared to be working out fine.

On that fateful day, we had attended church as usual, enjoyed a quiet dinner for three, and retreated to the family room for some Sunday afternoon rest. While my spouse snored softly in his recliner, Renee and I curled with our books in opposite corners of the couch. I was about to doze off when my couch partner suddenly erupted.

Screeching loud enough to break the sound barrier, she bounded from the couch. Clawing at her long dark hair, she squalled, "No! Get off me!" Dancing away from my soothing touch, she hollered, "Don't touch me! They'll get on you."

"I can't know what's going to get on me if you won't let me look."

The frenzied whirl and yell continued until her father finally thumped to his feet and bellowed, "Will you please quiet down and tell your mother what's wrong?"

My beloved has probably never bellowed more than a dozen times in his life. She stopped to stare.

"Daddy, I've got lice!"

I examined every inch of her shiny clean hair and found exactly five nits clinging somewhere between her right ear lobe and the nape of her neck. Her father broke the Sabbath long enough to drive down the hill and come back with a bottle of smelly liquid guaranteed to destroy lice; Miss Mother Teresa spent the rest of the day washing and rewashing her hair.

Come Monday, at my insistence, she quietly reported her "find" to her counselor. Relieved of further responsibility, knowing she had acted according to school rules, she went on to class.

However, our nitpicker being but one among several who had reported Traci's lice problem, her discretion meant nothing. When totally ticked Traci finally returned to school after two weeks of quarantine, she refused all further contact with the one who had so befriended her.

While those were tough days for our Good Samaritan, Traci's rejection served as a reminder that not everyone is receptive to the good we would do for them. And while gospel seed must continuously be sown, sometimes precious little of it will actually fall on fertile ground.

As for Traci, whether she ever realizes it or not, those nits fell on the head of a caring friend.

Lord, it's easy to ladle soup for an anonymous group, and to write checks. Help me to see and to serve the unlovely, one person at a time. Help me to serve with gladness no matter what the consequence.

Mom, Does God Know We're in Wyoming?

Picture a scene as familiar to Americans as a Lincoln penny—a cardboard sign nailed to the front of an ingenious array of apple (or orange or corrugated) boxes beneath giant elms (or honey locust or flowering cherry trees) lining a front sidewalk.

"Look, Mom, we made 24 (or 59 or a measly 17) cents," they exclaim at the end of a sultry morning throughout which paper cups of tepid lemonade—tepid due to the number of ice cubes one longsuffering refrigerator can produce—to passersby for the amazing price of three cents.

Considering the escalating price of the lowly lemon and sugar, and that overhead almost always must be absorbed by the grocery budget, to question true profit is valid.

Valid argument or not, this mom considers it more edifying to figure profit in happy hearts and satisfied grins than to worry over the cost of a lemon or even to fret over sticky floors and a cracked pitcher.

Chapter 42

Beautiful as a Mud Fence

Give thanks to the Lord, for he is good; his love endures forever.

—1 Chronicles 16:34, NIV

One would think Scouting might be high on the list of fun things to do for any active child. Not our seven year old.

"Too slow," she complained near the end of her first and only year as a Brownie Scout. "I like doing fast things."

Remembering her penchant for always taking an opposite view, I suggested, "Day camp will be different." Besides, five mornings of supervised activities at the park while I accompanied her dad on a brief business trip would mean fewer hours for her older sisters to try to cope with her unpredictable ways.

"No, it won't. They'll make me sit at a table with spilled ketchup and splintery benches and make junky stuff out of soup cans and ugly buttons. Please, don't make me go," she begged.

"Don't worry, Mom; we can handle it," the one presently working her way through practice teaching at the local junior high school insisted.

Sure enough, "She's hardly been out of the back yard since you left," a sibling reported when we phoned home that first evening to see how things were going.

A second phone call resulted in a similar report. "A lot of neighbor kids came over. They yelled all afternoon—some Tarzan thing they're playing—but they haven't been fighting."

Having gotten to know far too many of our neighbors through kid squabbles, we considered the peace report good news.

When we got home on Saturday, green loops of garden hose snaked suspiciously across the back yard and a new and mud-caked shovel lay beneath the peach tree. The main prop for the "Tarzan thing" masterminded by our second grader turned out to be a mud hole of old-fashioned pigpen proportion occupying the once-dry space beneath our oversized swing set.

"Watch me!" squealed our wiry little Tarzana as we stepped out onto the patio to survey the mess.

Monkeying up the sidebars, she untangled a rope fashioned ingeniously from old towels tied onto a faded pink crib sheet. Grasping a knotted end, she let out a Weissmuller yell and skimmed across the mud hole, her feet barely missing the twig-strewn water. After several such passes, she suddenly kicked off her thongs, let go of the makeshift rope, and dropped feet first into the hole, splattering mud in all directions.

"Tarzan falls sometimes," she explained, lifting her T-shirt to wipe splats of mud from an elfin face. Knee deep in a pool dug with diligence and pride, she was not prepared for anything other than applause.

True, we laughed. But weren't parents supposed to scold kids for making uncalled for messes? After all, she had "ruined" a good shovel and "spoiled" the ground beneath the swing set, to say nothing of "permanent" mud stains. And what had the neighbors thought as our mud dripped off their kids onto their clean floors?

In due time, the shovel got cleaned and oiled and hung in the garage, the mud hole filled, and the kid put to soak in the bath tub. I was doing dinner dishes when I quit muttering over the chaos in the laundry room long enough to lift my sights to the wide board fence marking the back of our property:

WELCUM HOM DADDY AN MOM. WE LOVE YOU AN MIST YOU.

Rivulets of mud had drizzled from the giant letters printed across the top boards onto the mud-scrawled names below—hers first, and then the correctly spelled names of all of her sisters. On the grass below, lying alongside an overturned mud-smeared sand pail, was my favorite paint brush, the slant-cut sash brush kept strictly for painting woodwork.

No rain happened to fall hard enough to damage her artwork and we never got around to painting the fence. For as long as we lived in that house, the message-in-mud served as a daily reminder that the unconditional love of a child is like that of our heavenly Father, whose steadfast love is not dependent on our response.

Further, while the Bible suggests heaping coals of fire onto opposing heads through acts of love, our knobby-kneed Tarzana achieved equally as much with a bucket of mud and a borrowed brush.

Lord, teach me to be so in tune with your ways that I will recognize your kind of love at a glance and learn to emulate it.

Chapter 43

Strike None

God is our refuge and strength, an ever present help in trouble. Therefore we will not fear.

—Psalm 46:1-2b, NIV

If we'd had no other reason for renting the old green-shingled house in the country with its weed patch of a garden, the swing was enough.

A marvel of fun-geared engineering, the swing began with a chain double-wrapped around the sturdy limb of a gnarled oak tree large enough for a bevy of small girls to hide behind without being seen (heard, probably, but not seen). While the chain appeared to our wide-eyed kids (and this five-foot-two mom) to drop like Jacob's ladder from the sky, in reality, the limb from which it hung grew several feet above the top of our bedroom window and a tad below the roof line of that two-story house.

You could take your pick among the swing seats we found leaning against the tree the day we moved in. Like the chairs in the story of the *Three Bears,* the smallest board had been cut just right for a child's wiggly bottom and the next size held two kids or one mom. Much too large for young children, the third seat had obviously been designed for the sort of moonlight swings Norm and I sometimes took after the kids had been prayed with and tucked into bed.

The swing worked nicely for pushing small children, and was also good for the kind of pumped-up, leveled-out jerking of chains that could suspend a stand-up *wunderkind* in stomach-stopping midair long enough to gray the hair of this longsuffering mother! Kids could dizzy themselves with twists and spins, slow swing with book in hand, or fight over their own bent rules for taking turns. Except for the birthday party at which ten kids argued for two hours over turns, the swing was a daily blessing, better than a baby sitter.

The night before the storm, as I cleared away supper things, I could hear the children giggling while their father gave pushes appropriate to courage and size and directed turns no one suspected would be the last.

A faint rumbling of thunder at bedtime, followed by distant flashes of lightning, suggested we could be in for one of the frequent storms common to Midwest summers. Rather than risk rain on our faces in the middle of the night, we lowered the upstairs windows to a crack, turned on the fan, and retired at our usual time.

Hours later, jerked upright by ricocheting balls of bluish light flashing outside our upstairs window, we listened with trepidation to the horrible rending and screeching sounds that preceded a giant crashing of thunder by a mere split second.

Bare feet skittered in the hall, the baby awoke and began to cry, and then I felt the tail of a seersucker nightgown swish across my face as our four-year-old clambered onto the bed and squeezed her plump body between us. The oldest grabbed the baby, the dark-haired one her blanket and, before any of us could say "lightning," our bed had turned into a nest of bawling, whimpering, frightened little girls.

"I will trust and not be afraid, Isaiah 12:2," the curly-haired one blubbered. Then, "Come on, you guys, say it with me. 'He careth for you.'"

"Sounded like lightning striking metal," their father explained after we'd obediently joined in repeating the verses we had helped them learn for Sunday school.

An hour or so later, after the children had finally gone back to sleep and the two of us were about as wide awake as we were likely to get, my spouse returned from a trip downstairs to report that lightning had struck the oak tree. "It's raining too hard to tell for sure," he said, "but I think it got the swing."

Next morning, what was left of the swing chain dangled from the stump of a limb that now lay across the driveway. Heat from the lightning had fused links in several places. Blackened splinters littered the back yard and goat pasture. Embedded in some were twisted links from the blown-apart chain. Shreds from what had once been sturdy swing seats hung like blackened corn silk from the hog wire fence separating yard and pasture.

Having grown up on a farm, I had seen cows killed by lightning and barns burned to the ground. What if a child had been sitting in the swing?

While the many storms that have since threatened our family have seldom been weather-related, the kids, as usual, were right. Because God cares for us as individuals and as a family, we have learned we need never be afraid.

Once in the middle of a storm at Grandma's, however, two who were at odds with each other laid aside their many differences long enough to cling to each other. What's more, they not only lived to tell about it, they eventually grew to become fast friends.

Lord, the swing incident was one time you protected us and we jolly well knew it. Thanks for all the times we've been unaware of your protection as you intercepted flak and rearranged circumstances to shield us from harm. Thank you for being a God who not only can walk on water but who stills our storms.

Our farmhouse stairwell with its large window lighting the first landing seemed a perfect place for a "time out" after our soon-to-be four-year-old had told an outrageous fib. The ten minutes in solitude, however, failed to kindle so much as a spark of contrition on the part of the short one.

"Who said telling lies is wrong?" she demanded to know as I opened the door to release her.

"God," I said before repeating what she and I both knew she had heard many times before. "The Bible is God's word and the Bible says lying is wrong. When we lie, we sin against God."

Her brown eyes flashed. "You know I don't have a Bible," she said. And in a teary tone, asked, "When are you going to buy me one?"

Chapter 44

Creepy Crawlers

The Lord detests the way of the wicked but he loves those who pursue righteousness.

—Proverbs 15:9, NIV

As frequent movers, we've met a lot of new neighbors over the years. We've also learned to recognize more than our share of new bugs. While at times certain of the kids leaned toward bugs—good, bad, or otherwise—I'll take neighbors anytime. Bugs were especially plentiful during the early years while we were renting.

There was the basement apartment. Come home at night, flip on the lights and, before anyone could blink, a zillion cockroaches scurried back to their cement block catacombs right before our eyes.

Open the back door of one house and a child grins at you from ear to tiny ear and asks you to take your pick from two fists full of night crawlers.

Open a back door in another place and discover that the floor where previous renters dumped food for cats has turned into a smorgasbord for a longer and larger breed of cockroaches. Think you've left cockroaches behind and, suddenly, you've got earwigs or still another variety of ants.

At one house, crickets devoured long slits and reduced to shreds the new pair of voile curtains I had just hung. In Illinois, silverfish ate holes in my wedding dress and we had mice. And, while mice are not bugs, they do give one the same creepy feeling.

My worst encounter with a creeping creature happened, not in a rental, but in the master bedroom of our first new house while standing before a full-length mirror trying on a new cream-colored dress. Noticing a large dark spot near the hemline, I reached down to pluck off what appeared to be a faded green raveling and met my first scorpion!

Then came spiders. Not ordinary, household spiders, or even the scary hairy oversized creatures we sometimes discovered beneath the eaves, but black widows. Scores of them.

It took no genius to figure out their origin. In our efforts to improve our unfinished back yard, we had fill dirt hauled in from the hills nearby. Now we needed to figure out how to get rid of the spiders and, until that happened, how to keep them from entering the house. While we quickly killed any black widow we saw both in and outside, we soon realized we were fighting a losing battle. Since the spiders had probably already laid eggs in the soil, to call an exterminator to spray house and grounds seemed an exercise in futility. Still, by the end of summer, our ruthless killings had reduced the population of other spiders as well as black widows. Next spring and early summer, the only black widows we saw appeared to be nesting near the back door. Come July, with time on her hands and a loathing for spiders, our determined junior higher declared war.

"I don't know how many cans of Raid I'm going to need," Renee told her dad, "but I hope you're paying for however many it takes." With that, she positioned herself on the back step, can in hand.

By noon the first day, she had killed nine.

The second day, she downed her breakfast and hit the step. "They're nesting under the shakes," she came in at ten to report. In order to blend with our hillside environment, the earth tone siding covering every house on our hill had been made with shakes. "They come out when the sun warms the shakes."

Since we had not seen a black widow elsewhere for quite some time, she was probably right. And, while the discovery made her job considerably easier, her spider hunt became no less time consuming. As the number of spiders decreased, she lengthened her "sit" until the day finally came when she announced, "I think I got the last of them."

She had indeed. For the five additional years we lived in that house, we never saw another black widow spider. Persistence had paid off.

And then she said, "I've spent so much time zapping spiders, I'm way behind on the Bible study I'm supposed to be doing for youth fellowship. Guess I'd better get busy on it."

Lord, when those things that displease you creep into our lives, be they one at a time or in hordes, arm us with the power of your word and provide us with the tenacity to do away with all that might hinder us in our walk with you. And Lord, thanks again for helping us get rid of those spiders.

"Mom," she sputtered the morning we disagreed over the attractiveness of a sweater she needed and had inherited from an older and bigger sister. "If you'd had a few boys before me instead of all girls, you wouldn't have to argue with me over all their dumb hand-me-downs."

Chapter 45

Search and Research

"Everything is permissible"—but not everything is beneficial. "Everything is permissible"—but not everything is constructive.

—1 Corinthians 10:23, NIV

Smacked with a shortage of credits on the last lap of her educational journey, our jolly one said not to worry. Rather than risk being handed an unsigned diploma, she would make arrangements to complete the required class through correspondence with one of our state universities.

Since she already carried a full load of classes and waited tables at a Chinese restaurant several evenings a week, we knew in advance what her solution to procrastination could entail. While her father and I worked on patience, the siblings sharpened their grumbling skills by taking turns doing her household chores along with their own. For her, the hours spent in reading and research turned out to be fun and the course was easy. Stil!, in spite of all we could do to help, to complete the paperwork in time for a mail-in deadline was not.

While living at home had its advantages, this daughter on the verge of leaving the nest had already started down the road toward independence. Realizing she genuinely had no time to do so, I offered to put an end to the disaster in her room by cleaning it. She turned me down.

"You've done enough already," she insisted. "I'll get to it."

She didn't, of course, and the litter deepened. Literally.

At the last possible minute, after every available inch had been captured by clutter, the inevitable happened. A paper disappeared. Not your ordinary paper covered with notes, or even a half-finished assignment due in one of her local classes. Oh, no. While attempting her best, she had not only buried the rest, but had lost track of a paper necessary for the completion of the correspondence course.

In the middle of a search that began on Monday as he was leaving to work out of town for the week, her father came home for the weekend. Our dependence on the paycheck that supported seven and paid school bills was no excuse. Before he could lift a foot over the threshold, it became his turn to show tangible concern—concern that soon turned into irritation.

"If you'd take a shovel and pitchfork to this room, you might be able to find something!" he fumed.

Eyes wide, the one aiming to graduate stared briefly at him. “But Daddy,” she wailed, “I’ve already looked under everything on the floor!”

Eventually, the paper got found and sent, her diploma signed and handed over to her—though not before we had all made a few observations.

Sure, it was her room and her stuff. If she chose to construct a disaster area, or even a 10” × 12” replica of the local city dump, that was her business. However, not all that is OK is necessarily to one’s benefit. What’s more, in prayer would likely have been a more edifying reason for an entire family to spend that much time on our knees.

Lord, I wonder how much of what clutters my days brings results in the form of a tardy response to your will for my life. Or, for that matter, hinders my family.

For the umpteenth time, the children had listened with interest to the story of Jesus blessing the children. As usual, the discussion centered around the rudeness of disciples who could be so calloused as to try to send the children away.

"I'll bet they wouldn't have said anything if it had been their *own* kids sitting on Jesus' lap," said our littlest.

Makes one wonder if we who strive daily to be like Jesus ever bother to make room in our hearts or our laps for a throwaway child or a kid who could use a good blessing but who does not belong to *us.*

Chapter 46

Socks Off

Train a child in the way he should go, and when he is old he will not turn from it.

—Proverbs 22:6, NIV

Living near the Wyoming gas fields in a town having a head count equal to the roster of a medium-size church had its limits. We had been there less than a year when we discovered one such limit had to do with the annual coercing of a student willing and/or equal to the awesome (to some) task of pronouncing the benediction for the junior-senior banquet program.

The class sponsor, a better-than-average English teacher (who happened also to be a weekend alcoholic), suffered regularly from Sunday indisposition. Had he been able to remain upright in a pew (doubtful), this pitiful shell of what must once have been a fine and sensitive man, was never about on Sundays to see who among his students attended church and who did not.

Reminding his students that he was not a prayer of prayers himself, he announced his need for a volunteer to his upper division classes and waited, but not for long.

On her way to her next class, Jennifer paused beside his desk and, without fanfare, said that she would be happy to conclude the banquet program with prayer.

Raising bushy eyebrows, the teacher squinted at her for a moment before offering a dubious, "All right. If you think saying a prayer is something you can do, jot down your idea of a prayer and show it to me."

Her eyes twinkled. "Is that an assignment?"

Disquieted, he shuffled some papers on his desk before replying, "No. But a prayer is. You want it to be just right, don't you?"

Her dimple deepened. "No problem. I can handle it."

Poor fellow. The possibility of a seventeen-year-old kid freelancing a prayer before half the student body being totally foreign to him, he worried.

Nevertheless, it was with growing concern that he detained the dimpled one at the close of class several times over the next few weeks to ask had she written her prayer. Her cheerful "No" never failed to provoke an admonishment to please do so lest she embarrass herself before her peers.

The day of the banquet dawned busy. I slid a twenty-four-pound turkey into the oven first thing and mixed a triple batch of Parker House rolls. At three o-clock, I put the rolls in to bake, carved and de-boned the turkey, shoved the pans filled with both into the car trunk, and drove to the school to help serve. Like I said, that wide-spot-in-the-sagebrush town had its limitations, including a shortage of stay-at-home junior class moms willing to bake rolls and de-bone turkeys.

The banquet went smoothly. The young people arrived looking their lovely or handsome best and quickly did away with almost all of the food a half-dozen mothers had spent two days preparing.

As the program, planned by juniors to honor seniors, drew to a close, I watched behind a cracked-open kitchen door as our daughter left her place at the now-cluttered table and walked the short distance to the podium. Clad in the white-over-pink lace sheath we had fashioned together, she looked poised and confident.

Not so, her teacher. It's hard to say if the expression dominating his once-handsome face had to do with stress over an unwritten prayer or with having been off the sauce since Sunday. Either way, he appeared apoplectic.

A mid-prayer peek at the same teacher, however, revealed the face of a man caught in the act of getting his socks totally knocked off by a prayer that turned out, not only to be beautiful, but appropriate for the listeners and precisely right for the occasion.

As the party broke up, the teacher first congratulated, then quickly accused her, "You wrote that prayer down and memorized it, didn't you?"

"No."

"You copied it."

"No."

"Oh, come on, yes, you did."

She looked him full in the face. "Why would I do that? I've been praying all my life. It's easy."

Poor man. Unless things have since changed, he may never believe or realize for himself that talking with God can be easier than speaking with a favorite teacher.

Or that you can "bring up a child in the way she should go and when she is sixteen or twenty, a mother, or even a grandmother, she will still know how to pray and will not be likely to depart from that privilege" (Proverbs 22:6, ALT [author's loose translation]).

Father, please, never let my children forget how to pray and help them to realize the importance of teaching their own children.

It has been said that little girls are made of "sugar and spice, and everything nice." If that is so, I wonder how our five managed to inundate us with so much pepper and "sass"…

Chapter 47

Imperfect Seven

Sons are a heritage from the Lord, children a reward from him...Blessed is the man whose quiver is full of them.

—Psalm 127:3-5, NIV

College commencement for our eldest had come and gone. Since none of the grandparents or other relatives had ventured west for the event, what better way to celebrate than to bundle our fledgling career candidate and her siblings into the car and go visit the older generation? "After all," we said to each other, "a chance to travel with all of our offspring in the same car may never happen again."

By the end of that trip, the kids' dad and I had perfected a tuneless, but brief and pointed duet: "I hope not."

While seven may well be the perfect biblical number, seven was no match for the interior of the only car we could afford at the moment, an aging blue Ford Galaxie. Two miles onto the freeway, and our engaged one begged to be returned to the arms of her fiancé, the graduate remembered a job she'd meant to apply for, and our college sophomore had forgotten her pillow. All that, mixed with one high school mouth and a kid determined to spread Tammy dolls over a back seat already occupied by antagonism in the flesh, signaled trouble before we'd driven past the first off-ramp into Boise.

Further, we had played tic-tac-toe for the last nine months while triple tuition wrestled for first place with our never-dwindling pile of other bills. With or without Tom Bodett's promise to keep Motel 6's lights on, to buy three motel nights for seven both going and coming was out of the question.

Thinking back, we should have taken note of God's travel plan for Abraham and Sara. Due to God's mapping out their lives by direct command, those two had ample time to get used to tent travel while they were still childless. Strapped as we were, we had to have been out of our minds to stuff a tent into a trunk alongside all the trappings girls were choosing to wear that summer instead of more practical blue jeans. With one opting for hot curlers, another rolling with juice cans, and two unable to share blow dryers (try all that in a tent site!), I gave thanks daily for the wee bag of pink rubber rollers that sufficed for our youngest.

Several car picnics, one windstorm, and a whole lot of hanging onto our patience later, we made it to our destination, all tempers intact. While the betrothed one squandered the last of her spending money on long distance calls, the rest of us relaxed and enjoyed several days with the grandparents before squeezing back into the Galaxie for a much shorter drive. The minute we rolled to a stop in the shade of an Illinois farm barn, our young adult children turned instantly back into kids.

Once the aunts, uncles, and cousins who hadn't seen each other in a while became a houseful, the men got in the pickup and went to have a look at the crops. While my sister-in-law and I snapped beans in the kitchen, the younger set spilled out onto the lawn. Following a brief discussion, the host kids took off for the barn and saddled the pony.

So small the taller kids could straddle her without using a stirrup, the pony was also tame. The graduate, however, still clung to a fear of animals that began at age two after a blind old dog accidentally walked into her in the dark. She agreed to give horsemanship a try only after her sisters had each had a couple of plodding turns around the house, beneath the clothesline, and back to the garage.

Possibly the pony sensed her fear. Could a ninth passenger on a sizzling July afternoon constitute overload? Either way, the long-suffering pony did a quick altering of gaits from plod to trot to canter, jerked to a stop, then made a fast turn. Not knowing how to handle the change in rhythm, the inexperienced rider panicked and fell off.

Snorting, the pony pranced beyond the reach of the boy cousins and stopped to sniff the ground near the fallen one. Fear having outdistanced pain, certain she was about to be trampled into lawn fertilizer, the now void-of-all-dignity graduate failed to notice that her left arm hung limp.

Called to the scene, we moms knew a broken arm when we saw one. We also recognized a circus.

Tired of putting up with kids, the horse kept its distance, circling harmlessly beneath the clothesline, keeping out of reach of the two boy cousins chasing after her.

The girls, meanwhile, having all studied first aid from different teachers, sought to assist the one with the broken arm.

"Find a stick and make a splint!" one hollered, while another insisted the arm be kept mobile.

"*Im*mobile, dummy. You don't move a broken arm," said an older sibling.

While girls leapt like Baal's prophets around the injured one, the advice continued.

"Use a towel and make a sling."

"Place it on a pillow and hold it like a purse."

Agreeing the pillow might provide both support and comfort, we gently held the pillow as we helped the injured one into the car and drove to the hospital. After examining the arm, a merciful doctor looked at two harried moms, considered the combined nine-kid household, and ordered a night's stay in the hospital before releasing our, by now, embarrassed graduate for further travel.

A grandmother loaned the middle one a pillow and the bride-to-be counted miles in minutes all the way home. Tammy and her rabble-rousing doll friends got banished to the trunk, and the high school all-mouth felt sorry enough for the one whose arm now itched beneath its cast to shut up. After enduring one all-night thunderstorm, damp beds, 104-degree weather, and shower faucets that had to be held on (try that with one arm in a sling!), we gave up on the last night of our homeward trip and stayed in a motel.

Looking back, laughing together over inconveniences that were not one bit funny at the time, we're still glad we made that trip. And while the Ford turned out to be less spacious than that biblical quiver, we were right; a trip for all seven of us never happened again.

Further, the best way to celebrate succeeding graduation milestones seemed to be with cake and punch.

Lord, while the saying is true that "families are forever," those same families are together under the same roof—and in the same crowded car—for only a few short years. Thank you, Father, for the gift of memories—the bad, the good, the funny, and the funnier—for it is a gift that helps pave the path to contentment long after the nest is empty.

Chapter 48

Chain Labor

Guard the good deposit that was entrusted to you—guard it with the help of the Holy Spirit who lives in us.

—2 Timothy 1:14, NIV

Like most families, we have our collection of heirlooms—a scarred wooden sugar bucket, Great-grandma's brass school bell, my husband's childhood chair with its split hickory bottom, and more. We also have the gum wrapper chain.

Long before the dark-haired one began working on the gum wrapper chain, she (and we) began collecting chewing gum wrappers. At the time, each stick of gum came encased in an individual wrapper complete with logo. Unlike today's plain inside wrap, each brand, right down to its paper-lined foil, bore a wrapped personality all its own. Beeman's Black Jack came wrapped in blue; Yucatann, in yellow and pink. Those, along with

Big Red, Juicy Fruit yellow, and the green-and-white wrappers from off Wrigley's mint flavors, soon filled a cigar box.

She began the braid with very little ceremony. She simply sat on her bed and folded those small rectangles together so they came out looking a little like braided rickrack. No, she didn't need any help. Please, would I make her sisters take their advice and their offers to help and get out.

For weeks after school, the braiding took precedence over everything else. We had to remind her of chores and homework and, at times, speak firmly before she would leave her project long enough to eat.

The day finally came when she emerged from the bedroom triumphant. Flinging the gum wrapper chain out straight on the floor, she flopped onto her back and stretched full length beside it.

"Is it long enough?" she asked her sister. "Is it as long as I am tall?"

It was.

The gum wrapper chain, it seems, needed to be her exact size, though not really. The fact was she and Dennis (the boy she currently liked) happened to be the same height. Made up of wrappers folded to form a length to match a boy's height, according to current teenage girl tradition, the gum wrapper chain was considered symbolic of undying adolescent love.

After carrying the gum wrapper chain to school for several days, she draped it across the top of the bulletin board in the room she shared with her sister. Being in the habit, we continued giving her our gum wrappers, as did her friends.

Typical of eighth grade romance, the time came when she stopped liking Dennis and began answering phone calls from Ron. While the gum wrapper chain no longer mattered, she did not discard it. She had worked too hard and long to make it.

I don't know when her younger sister began adding gum wrappers, but there came a day when the gum wrapper chain got thumbtacked to the ceiling and hung clear to the floor. Next, the two agreed that, by working together, the chain might eventually encompass the upper perimeter of their room.

Some time along, I noticed that working on the gum wrapper chain had therapeutic value. Through folding bits of paper, a kid could cool down after a "mad" or work through disappointment. For the tired or cranky, an hour of "chain labor" proved as good as a nap.

We moved before the chain quite reached around the room where it had gotten its start. The chain went along and, as the girls grew older, passed from hand to hand. By the time the youngest of the siblings had been granted permission to add on to the chain, most manufacturers had switched to plain inner wrappers and those bright wrappers with logos had gotten harder to get.

The gum wrapper chain no longer circles a room, but lies coiled in a good-sized box at the home of our fourth-born. While the chain may be useless, it has also become a collector's item too good to throw away. I know this is true, because I've seen one among other collector's items in a well-known museum. I know nothing of those who folded the gum wrappers used to form that twenty-inch gum wrapper chain (puny, compared to ours), or what that particular creation means to its former owner. Perhaps, as does ours, certain sections of that chain could bring back memories to those who worked on it.

Our gum chain, I think, symbolizes the strength and endurance and continuity of family. As God has woven the tapestry of each of our lives, he has also braided us together in a never-ending chain of shared events and spiritual ups and downs.

Lord, the journey continues to be a precious one. Thanks! We wouldn't have missed it for anything.

Printed in the United States
55379LVS00001BA/2